HUMANITY RISING

A Journey from Fear and
Control to Love and Freedom

Dr Nicky Hamid

Professor of Happiness

Ascension Reminder Series

Humanity Rising

© 2021 by NICKY HAMID (MA.,Ph.D., Dip Tchg)

All rights reserved. No part of this publication may be reproduced, stored in a retrieval system, or transmitted by any means – electronic, mechanical, photographic (photocopying), recording, or otherwise – without prior permission in writing from the author.

Printed in the United States of America.

ISBN: 9798471686670

Learn more at: http://www.globalmissionoflove.com

Testimonials

Emma - Thank you for giving me pause to think about how the divine interlaces itself with our reality. Through your work I have been lifted up many times to see myself and others with a new lightness of being. You inspire me. - Melbourne Australia –

Jocelyn You have given me hope when I just wanted to believe that there was no good left in the world. But, your messages help me remember that the good actually outweighs the bad and we are the ones that have to show the rest of the world. - Chicago, IL USA.

Aneta Always a Thank You! Your words help me to remember indeed, there is a resonance and it feels true when I read them. It helps me to keep some orientation and grounding in these chaotic times. It helps to feel more centred again. It helps to access my own inner knowledge. Often your posts tell exactly what I need to hear. And that love that shines through your posts, so beautiful! Very grateful that you are here and support us! Thank you! – New England. USA

Kathleen I found your FB page at the exact moment that meditation began to be more than just a random practice for me. Through your posts I have received guidance to deepen my meditation practice but so much more! I am truly grateful for the beautiful and kind space you have created. Nearly every morning your posts are the first I see and your words seem to speak PRECISELY to something in me... I feel supported and cared for by a global circle of love! - Florida, USA

Sirpa I am a Finn. Your writings always bring me peace, that I am ok. I understand now that it is ok to be me and that I don't have to follow or aim to be like any of my "teachers" because I am here and now because of me and quite unique. – Finland.

.... and hundreds more ....

Dedication

This book is dedicated to all my facebook friends and followers who, by their sincere and honest participation, have contributed in a very real way to the energy behind the words.

One Huge Soul Family

Table of Contents

Introduction How to Use this Book. 1

Chapter 1 A View Some Time After the End Times (2012).. 6

Chapter 2 How You are Making a Difference. 9

Chapter 3 Choice, and Feeling your Freedom 11

Chapter 4 The Rite of Passage for Humanity 13

Chapter 5 One New Breath 15

Chapter 6 Befriending Your Ego 17

Chapter 7 A Simple View of You as Creator 20

Chapter 8 On Inspiring ("Helping/Healing") Others. 23

Chapter 9 A Myth Buster 26

Chapter 10 Going Beyond the Shared Human Trauma 28

Chapter 11 You are the Gift You bring to the World 30

Chapter 12 The Unravelling of Collective Programmes 32

Chapter 13 The Healing of Humanity 33

Chapter 14 Deepen You Relationship with Gaia 36

Chapter 15 Living with Frequency Focus 38

Chaper 16 The Divine Mystery Revealed Perhaps? 40

Chapter 17 Ego Points the Way 42

Chapter 18 Meditate, Meditate, Meditate 45

Chapter 19 On Being Bold. 47

Chapter 20 The Great Shining is Here 49

Chapter 21 You are Living on the Cutting Edge: JUMP 51
Chapter 22 Living from a 5th Dimensional State 53
Chapter 23 Creating Your New Earth Experience............... 55
Chapter 24 Moving from Logic to Feeling. 58
Chapter 25 Cutting the Cords to Old Ways of Thinking. 60
Chapter 26 End Game: The Real Conspiracy – (Part I) 62
Chapter 27 End Game Part II: Weapons of Mass Distraction 64
Chapter 28 From Sacred Heart: A Field of Flowers............ 68
Chapter 29 From Chaos to Peace 70
Chapter 30 Mother Love 72
Chapter 31 Anger Management 74
Chapter 32 Many Hearts One Trajectory. 76
Chapter 33 The Power You have to Make a Change for All. 78
Chapter 34 Share Who You are with Realistically. 80
Chapter 35 Toward Unity in Galactic Consciousness 82
Chapter 36 Set Yourself Free.. 84
Chapter 37 Your Purpose is to Love Being You. 86
Chapter 38 World Peace: How can it be Attained?............. 88
Chapter 39 Your Right to be Happy 90
Chapter 40 Some Keys for Creating. 92
Chapter 41 Moving from Limitation to Freedom................ 94
Chapter 42 Becoming Unattached.. 96
Chapter 43 A Look into Who You are in Essence as HUman

.... 98

Chapter 44 Divine YOU is Always Present if You Allow 99

Chapter 45...Shining a light on Shadow................................. 101

Chapter 46 A Declaration as a Citizen of Earth. 103

Chapter 47 Embracing Our "Younger" Warriors of Light . 104

Chapter 48 Your World Needs You 107

Chapter 49 A New Way of Being 109

Chapter 50 Finding Your True Love 111

Chapter 51 Creating a New World Together........................ 113

Chapter 52 How to Master these Times. 115

Chapter 53 Finding the Courage to be Vulnerable. 117

Chapter 54 Love to Places of Conflict in Our World.......... 119

Chapter 55 We "Fell" Because We Ignored our Heart Knowing. 121

Chapter 56 The Joy in following Your Heart....................... 123

Chapter 57 The Mastery of Non-Judgement 124

Chapter 58 The Wisdom of the Human Collective. 125

Chapter 59 Time to Step Up 127

Chapter 60 Standing Firmly in Embodiment, I AM 129

Chapter 61 Clearing the 'Past'. 131

Chapter 62 Be Still "I Am God". 134

Chapter 63 The Gift of You 136

Chapter 64 On Inspiring ("Helping") Others. 139

Chapter 65 Straight Talk, to Precious Soul that You Are... 142

Chapter 66 At Home with the Ups and Downs of Life 144

Chapter 67 Lighten Up 145

Chapter 68 A Word on "Ascension". 146

Chapter 69 All the Old Stuff is Leaving if You will Allow. 148

Chapter 70 Stop Scaring Yourself 151

Chapter 71 We All Have Ever Changing Stories 153

Chapter 72 To Look for Inspiration Daily 155

Chapter 73 Living in Your New Reality 157

Chapter 74 The Creative Power We have for Good 159

Chapter 75 To Love Fearlessly 161

Chapter 76 Seeking Presence with Others and in Yourself. 163

Chapter 77 Understanding How You May Affect Others.. 165

Chapter 78 Duality as Opportunity to Experience Choice. 167

Chapter 79 On the Way and Always Home 169

Chapter 80 Quantum Entanglement 171

Chapter 81 The Gift of Sharing 173

Chapter 82 The Rising of Compassion. 175

Chapter 83 Happiness as a Way of Life. 177

Chapter 84 An Activation: Old Habits Die Hard. 178

Chapter 85 Changing Your Frequency of Experiencing.... 181

Chapter 86 When Your Light Switches On 183

Chapter 87 Behind Every Stone is Something New 185

Chapter 88 No Other Authority Above Your Own Truth. 188

Chapter 89 The Greatness of You Being Here 190

Chapter 90 All Our emotions are essential to Being Human 192

Chapter 91 Healing Through Shifting Emotions 194

Chapter 92 Feeling More of Who You Are 196

Chapter 93 Pure Love. 198

Chapter 94 On Living the Dream 200

Chapter 95 Love Unstoppable 202

Chapter 96 Standing Sovereign Together. 204

Chapter 97 Find and Express Your Joy. 206

Chapter 98 Disengaging from the 3D "Movie". 209

Chapter 99 POSTSCRIPT 211

About the Author 212

Contact Information 214

Readers Note Pad 215

Introduction
How to Use this Book.

One of the premises on which this book is written is that there is no such thing as an accident. The unexplained and the unexpected is one of the essential characteristics of our experiencing life and if we can accept that we do not have to know everything to live fully, then we can allow for the unknown to be a part of how we will experience life.

So the fact that you are reading this book is no accident. You have picked up a token of energy that is connected to all that the words are connected to, and those words stand for an expression of my knowing as the writer. There is something in this book for you otherwise you would not have been drawn to it or picked it up in the first place.

So if you decide to read on then make some intent to be open to whatever it is that you need that the words, the ideas will trigger within you. My views, my ideas, my point of view is only that, my view. I do not consider what is contained in my work represents any definitive or absolute Truth. I believe that each reader will have their own working truth and therefore I know that you will read and take unto yourself only that which resonates with you. However, be careful not to discard what you do resonate with, if you come to anything you cannot go along with, just put those parts aside to examine, or not, at a later date.

Furthermore, it is important not to accept what I say as true just because I say it. Be aware that if you find things that make sense to you and helps you, that the truths therein were really already yours. It was that you were just not consciously aware of them up till now.

This book is about waking up or remembering things that you have long forgotten, have dismissed, or have bypassed in your need to keep your footing in these chaotic times, and it is my greatest joy if what you read here can help you remember.

As you read do trust yourself, and if questions arise, trust that the answers will be given to you. Sincere seeking will always be satisfied if you stay open. Just as you have been led to this book for something it can spark in you, your quest for understanding will be met through many avenues, events and people. So enjoy the trip we will make together as you read, along with all the energy and knowing of those who have read this work before you.

This is not a book that you read from cover to cover in a few sittings. It is a workbook, a kind of modern oracle.

It primarily contains short reminders, memory joggers, heart activators that will set movements, mini shifts in your perception, knowing and feelings. Therefore, I strongly advise that you do not read any more that two of the entries at any one sitting.

Three ways to use this book

Read the 99 chapters (reminders) in the powerful sequence they are already written in, and for which you are going to be surprised how often they fit perfectly into circumstances you are experiencing at the time of your reading.

Cut out ten cards of equal size using light cardboard. Write a number from 0 to 9 on each card. You can them use these cards as your deck. Shuffle the deck and choose a card. That will be your first number. Replace the card in the deck, reshuffle and choose a second card. This will give you the number of the reading for that day. The single digit numbers will have a "0" in front of them. Use the "00', when it occurs, as a wild card that allows you to choose any chapter that appeals to you from the Table of Contents.

Or simply, at each reading time, trust in your own innate process and open the book at random and read that section that has been "chosen for you" as it were.

If you believe and trust in the power of your intent then any of these procedures will be highly fruitful. It is really all about Trusting in your own inner process and in a certain "magical" relationship that develops between you and the readings.

How the Energy of this Book Works

When you choose your reading it is very important that you choose without thought. The reading will then reflect what your Soul knows is a most helpful direction for you to respond to. You then begin to get answers through the phrases and the words, and the feelings and the sounds of Love being transmitted into yourself. They awaken and create a vibration of resonance (remembering) in your self-realising.

Your Soul drives your choice and you connect through your eye-brain and directly into your endocrine system, initiating feelings. and shifts that are palpable.

You will often find that the reading connects to the last dream you have had or a very recent or upcoming event. They connect you to the current journey you are taking and align with an understanding that will be most empowering for you.

Using the Book regularly, at least for a period of sequential days, will help you to connect the dots to your own creative lineage and the undoing of the knots that have bound you to shadows. At the same time you will be building a foundation of Love that will hold you safe in your unsettling dreams, and through events, to be able to "rise" quickly through your fear, and self-doubt.

Frequent daily reading is building up a relationship between your own unique frequency and that of the Truths behind each reading. You will quickly develop a personal resonance from which grows your own capacity to receive the shifts and beautiful profound insights ("ahas"), that are part of your innate wisdom.

You come into this incarnation with thought forms you have previously created. The readings act directly on raising these thought forms to dissolves them. You can achieve this so easily by acknowledging what a reading has brought up in you, allowing it to be there and saying "Yes, Yes. Thank you, thank you. Now I Know."

Thus in the Knowing, it is over and the end of the "story" because you remembered the experience without attaching it to a fear story or an unkind lie thought.

When you use the book in this way you are going to receive teachings that will bring to you truth that is current for you. And that truth is that you come into incarnation as your own Being, with your thought forms, and your Being (Soul) will sing to you that which is to be dissolved and changed.

And the song of your Being sings, through the book, the next thought form that frees you as you choose your daily reading. Most of these thought forms are unconscious, and if after the reading you feel them and give them no more story, the deprogramming is complete. The loop of recreating the future from the past is broken because it is now where it was created, in the conscious mind itself.

Thus as you do the regular reading, guided by your Soul, you are having an interaction and the most Loving guided elevated dialogue with SELF. A dialogue that allows the dissolving of that which you clearly see as not holding the Sound of Love.

When you read many of the readings in this book, you are going to receive self-realisations. Through the fire of your awakening you will dissolve the distortions that are repressing your own Light from rising. And this change, this transforming, this healing is INSTANT.

Use of a Postscript

You will see that many of the readings have a postscript "**PS:**" at the end

This supports the theme of the main body of text but in addition supplies some help note that enable you to either relate the reading more specifically to your own circumstances or further reinforces and strengthens the relevance of the ideas for you.

CHAPTER 1

A View Some Time After the End Times (2012)

The mesmerising power of duality reality is fading fast. Earth is at peace with herself and the changes She is making now only reflects back the 3D confusions in the minds of human outer collective consciousness. But the Human contingent, from its willful slumber, has been hard to rouse. It appears that everything 'man made' is crumbling and outdated. Fears arise and obstruct most people from letting go of the old ideas and habits of thought.

Minds are confused and cannot get their heads around anything that is not familiar or simple in conception. Emotions are rampant, easily provoked, and out of proportion, and with little or no outer connection to the trigger events.

Bodies ache and are tired, and are most inclined towards long and frequent hibernation, and pain numbing habitual addictions.

Linear Time continues to accelerate as we have moved away from the 2012 Snapshot point for the New Reality.

As the pressure of the ages accelerates, the surfacing of all that is not in alignment with Love and integrity of Being rises to be acknowledged and dealt with as a conscious release for every individual.

The Pressure is enormous and relentless on the human subconscious, subliminal psyche.

There is no hiding, each person's Truth Contract must be honoured in some way. And for those of you who have released much, there is the reality of Unconditional Loving that pervades your perception, knowledge and feeling.

The release is occurring through You at a rapid pace, but mostly you can be calm if you daily make that choice.

Even the outbursts are quick, and if allowed to play themselves out if neither the need to know any ins or outs, nor to attach any great significance to any of it. To see it all like a Loving parent watching, with Smile, at an altercation between two children. Love is within and about All and the monumental releasing is affecting everyone.

Thus in your Lovingness the old world is fading fast for many, apart from unreal appearances to the contrary playing out in the external "movie". For others it is only a matter of becoming confident, to let go all doubts, and allow all that is internal to play itself out in the external world and to buy into none of it. To analyse none of it, and to watch it fade, while the Love that You are, by your very Nature, grows. In your Shining you will be there for others but you must also allow others to live the reality they choose without judging or being drawn into "right" or "wrongness".

Love them anyway. Less is more.

Peace in the Human Heart, through the Divine Light Weaving Wave that is permeating everything and everyone, and is descending on Earth within form and physicality. Within You.

Simply ALLOW.

PS: Your "Truth Contract", is your Soul undertaking which might go something like this. .... "I am here, to complete this phase of my journey in form, with Openness, Honesty, and Love with and for myself, through all experiences, as an embodiment of Source. To bring and hold LIGHT. A Brilliant Soul Light of Infinite Possibility and Eternal Lovingness".

CHAPTER 2

How You are Making a Difference.

You see all the things going on in the world and sometimes doubt the power of your Lovingness to change what is happening. Even though you cannot see the impact you are making, be assured that the Company of Heaven stand in awe of the changes we are making as a HUman Collective.

And to You who are awakening early and are discovering the real power of Lovingness, the reason we are seeing all the disruption in our lives, the lives of all around us, and on the Planet, is because you have made an impact and in your own stirring have stirred things up.

You have raised questions and have made people question, each in their own way (your powerful Heart powered thoughts are "in the ethers, the quantum field, for others to pick up on).

And now things cannot be hidden as they once were. Secrets cannot be kept and thus you are seeing everything that has been done, that was hidden, and that is out of integrity with what humans truly are, is coming to Light.

All who are in "power' who think they have some responsibility for others lives are becoming answerable to what they have done, what they think, and what they now do. And thus you see governments, "authorities' floundering, inept, "frightened" and in great dysfunction, whenever they are out of alignment with the wills and true wellbeing of the people.

All of the disruption is the result of your Love creating and enlivening a Light Frequency into the Collective Consciousness that will not allow this "negativity" to continue in the status quo.

HUmanity is being called by you, through your Love of who you are as Human, to Wake Up as you are doing in your personal life.

So Beloved Brothers and Sisters, you are having a huge effect on the change and transformation in human affairs which is well underway.

And do not forget that, as you transform your world, as you find it, through your inner reflection and perception, and take mastery of yourself in your daily life, it ripples out to touch everyone.

You are that powerful.

Again, through owning your Lovingness and discerning what thoughts are yours and which ones are not. Which thoughts you choose to keep and which you do not. In doing so you are bringing into being the frequencies which are totally in line with the Divine Flow (because this is where your attention and intention is) and which is transforming everything in human affairs.

You "set an example" to follow, you open "the door", you become the open door, for others to find their own way through.

Shine On.

PS: Live your own life fully, touch where you can and where you are guided, and view all else from a point of neutrality without fear or judgment. And thus we will all play our part in the Amazing Great Plan of Change creating a New Golden Age here on Earth.

CHAPTER 3

Choice, and Feeling your Freedom

Of course, you experience pleasant and unpleasant, irritation and exhilaration, light and dark, sadness and joy, and the infinite differences of this and that, here and there, now and then.

Of course, you are experiencing choice points all the time.

However, as you are waking up, your reliance on subliminal and habitual choice making has to go.

You are here to experience contrasting frequencies and to master them as yourself.

And have you not realised that it is in the feeling of choice that freedom is experienced.

All this is Beautiful Human, is an awesome wonder of embodiment here on Earth.

But who is it that is experiencing all this?

Who is experiencing the freedom to choose or experience this or that?

It is YOU the "Watcher", the Lover, the continuous ever present SOUL BEING You are, "the in between", the BEING OF SOURCE. The You that is neither this nor that.

It is You that Just IS, unceasingly, eternally, universally Present.

You are the Presence, the Shine, the unfathomable, Love Beingness.

You are a unique expression of God.

CHAPTER 4

The Rite of Passage for Humanity

Now are the Times of a "right of passage", an Initiation of the consciousness of HUmanity as a whole.

Issues of addressing oppression, racism, injustice, equality and compassion are coming up for each of us to face in our own way. Facing up to it personally and collectively.

To let go of what needs to be let go of. To be nudged, cajoled, inspired, and pushed over the edge from the familiar into the unknown.

Everyone in their own way senses the huge Change coming from deep within themselves and from the chaos, the shaking up of the collective psyche going on all around the planet.

What has been in human affairs was never enough. Collectively we have had enough of being victim. Thus people are standing up in terms of opinion. No longer able to suppress the deep discontent.

A Revolution in consciousness that is brewing in the masses is flooding out from the wounded Heart into the streets and market places.

We have had enough of what was Humanity, and people can no longer ignore or pretend, or maintain their resigned silence that what was is all there is They are beginning to consider and are making a decision that what could be must be.

Change is desired but how, who, what, and when are often misguided as people grapple with the hurt of ages.

Look closely and you will find it happening everywhere.

A revolution (evolution) in Consciousness. Increase protest, increase asking questions, increased confusion, increased push to "change", and the increased merging of exchanges and sharing, exploration and creative innovation of "grassroots" experiments for something new, something Heart based, going on all around the world in a 100,000 small communities and villages. An Amazing "groundswell that silently and stealthily is expanding.

And it all starts with you and I.

First within finding your LOVE.

And Second through sharing Your LIGHT... through your New Earth Dream and Visions, as you discover and uncover your Soul Family both here in physicality and in your Now Present Company of Heaven.

We no longer have to do it on our own. Nor is it possible or necessary.

It is in the accelerating transformation of consciousness that is happening to us all.

CHAPTER 5

One New Breath

The only constant in the Universe is CHANGE.

You asked for change. You yearned for an entirely new way of human expression. And now it is here for everyone, and you still feel stuck? As though nothing is changing and the old reality remains bringing up all that you thought would be gone?

But it has 'gone'. It no longer has any basis to maintain and sustain itself. There is no energy to support it.

It is only your habits of doing and patterns of perceiving and reacting that are keeping the illusion going.

In the old, Humans always looked for the familiar and clung to it even though it was painful and debilitating. We see it happening all around us.

So now you are cut adrift, knowing of your Divinity, feeling the magnetism of the New, the synchronous and the miraculous, but still feeling pulled back to the old at almost every turn.

So what to do?

Stop putting yourself down and everything around you. Let go, let go, let go.

Step out of the duality habits of thought and feeling by becoming the watcher (neutral point). And in this Being, Love comes, Love is there.

Begin to consciously breathe into every moment the New Breath. The Flow of Love from deep within, of the truth of You that you ARE right Now. And this is the Reality of where we now stand.

Even though you might live in situations where old patterns appear to flourish, breathe NEW BREATH and watch the change happen.

Watch it change in you, in circumstances, and in others.

Watch the changes happen without any effort on your part, except your Loving Breath.

Even old circumstances become new, free and unfolding conditions.

What was, is no longer.

Stop preconceiving it or other people as though it/they are still as you once knew it/them to be.

In Infinite possibility everything becomes new.

PS: WE breathe between 18000 to 30,000 breaths per day. All you need to take is 300 conscious breaths a day and you will transform your life and everything around you.

Try sitting for 10 minutes just being with your breath. No heavy focus just saying "IT breaths me. GOD, the Golden Light of Creation breaths me."

If your mind wanders just simply come back to breath and continue.

And while moving in your day, every time you think of it breathe in golden Light, through the top of your head into your body, like a waterfall.

Receive and breathe that golden LIGHT out into your field.

In 21 days you will be a different person, you will feel more powerfully, more confident within YOU.

CHAPTER 6

Befriending Your Ego

It is extremely easy to understand your ego.

Everything in all Creation, including You, are in constant movement. Change, flux, movement, spin, in and out, is the name of the game of Creation.

Ego wants nothing more than for you than to remain where you are. In the safest place it has found for you. It wants static, familiar, inertia, safe, certainty, control, predictable, expected.

Change, any change, is uncomfortable, unpredictable, unknown, and scary for the ego.

Ego says to all change "Warning, Danger, effort, uncomfortable, threatening to me. Don't go there. It is far better to stay where you are". "Think about it", "check it out first". " Ignore it, hide yourself from it".

When you know you need to change something but are saying you do not know how to change it, then you do not want to change, you are postponing the inevitable change.

You are of SOURCE.

You CANNOT BE CONTAINED.

And as a Soul Being in HUman form you have been given the most Precious gift....FREEWILL.

You are the change, and you are continually able to change, but you (ego you) simple is coming up with excuses for you not to be able to do what you are capable of in any given moment. What your Soul Being is asking of you.

You are being called to step into the VOID, but all your ego can do is nag you to AVOID doing it. Ego digs up your past fear experiences.

How willing are you to change, to go with your own Flow of change?

It is Will, your will that is the key.

Your CHANGE comes from the choice to take hold of The Divine, Essential, Expansive, Knowing WILL of YOU, navigated through Heart direction, REGARDLESS of the warnings of ego.

YOU are the CHANGE you have been waiting for.

It is time to put to rest forever the "illusionary safety of little mind" (ego self).

Let Change, New, Fresh, Clear, Expansive be your journey.

Rest in Peace Beloved ego.

Be still that I may fly FREE.

PS: Understand that your ego is not your enemy. It has been your fail-safe. It lets you know immediately whenever you are out of alignment with who you truly ARE. It points to you the conscious choice you are having to make in order to stand FREE.

BEFRIEND YOUR EGO. Teach it to rest NOW because the WAR in yourself is over. It has done its job and you are so grateful for how it is pointing always to your Truth calling.

PPS: The bottom line is......

You cannot get rid of EGO. It is actually your great benefactor as Beautiful HUman.

In your life circumstances at the moment, are you being ask to choose between....... the 'devil' that you know rather than the God that you don't?.......... Or the unkind thought lies of outer programming, versus the Truth that you Know in your inner Feelings and Heart Knowing.

Stay the course dear reader. WE are building a NEW HUman consciousness dynamic. Each through our daily conscious Freewill Choices.

CHAPTER 7

A Simple View of You as Creator

Change your thoughts and you change your world.

Thoughts are creations. Each thought forms an imprint on quantum-like packets of information that you have "crystalised" as it were. It is available in the quantum field for everyone just like radio waves are available. But thoughts are not neutral.

As a human being, each thought is wrapped (magnetised) through the feeling tone that goes with it from your sense experience at the time of its creation, beliefs, values, interests, intentions. Each thought then attracts or is attracted to other's thoughts that resonate with it and thus our reality is constructed (formed), like a fluctuating coagulated representation of your thought/feeling creation.

And thus the reality you see and experience (eg 3D) is a temporary ever changing expression of what you are attracting to you through your projections into the 3D field.

And remember thoughts are all of the past. You are seeing what WAS created by your thoughts a moment or more ago. You can only create in your next Now and it exists as a potential of your "future" Now.

As we are waking up it becomes evident that what you experience is not going to alter unless you think differently, and you are not going to significantly alter your thought projections and manifestations, your reality, unless you change the feelings you experience about Life as you find it Now. And you are not going to experience, nor create anything with the feeling tones you yearn for unless you first take hold and Master your feeling tones in each Now moment.

This is why your imperative for Living and creating Now is for you to become more and more attentive to your "Inner", your own process. Your intuitive navigational compass, your Heart Knowing, your Love of and for who you are, and your active state of Lovingness (5D).

So simply.

You go within and feel the Field of you, the LIGHT FIELD in the background of your Lovingness. Then you begin to consciously choose (create) to experience anything in your Life that aligns with this. You start to deliberately and consciously stop, listen, and watch until you become aware of feelings of wholeness and "isness". From here you start to experience the tone of your Lovingness.

Then, and only then, can you look at the "external" and begin to see it in a new, fresh enlivened way. And finally you can create the thoughts that will carry this tone into your reality. Your reality experience is a reflection of the Love/Light tone you intentionally choose, in any given moment.

Your Being is calling you to sing another song, but You, and only You can create it. Where your attention goes your energy Flows.

And this is why I recommend that you give up ALL your stories that relate to a reality that you are finished with. Things just do not work in the old ways. There is just not the energy to support the old structures. The HUman Collective has finished with it.

Allow the Old reality to fade and dissolve, put your attention elsewhere, (and this is not a shutting off from things you do not like) and let the New Reality emerge through your consciously adopted feeling tone.

PS: And of course I know that you know all this. But at whatever level you have read this, there are clues in your resonance with these words for your next steps.

CHAPTER 8

On Inspiring ("Helping/Healing") Others.

First and foremost, if you are in your Shining, in your Presence, then you have already brought the greatest gift you could to those you are in the company of.

In your countenance, your smile, through your eyes and from your heart, comes the magic of Flow which even a fractional part can be known full well by others. And thus in essence there is nothing to do, nothing that has or needs to be said for The Gift to be given. It can pass "unseen and unheard", but felt, heart to heart.

When I first started my counselling and therapy work, over 50 years ago, I resolved to trust my training to the Universe and trust the "patient/client" to bring to me what they needed for me to help them with, and to trust myself that what I did would lead to the most benevolent outcome for all concerned.

I cannot remember it ever not working for me.

There was no system or theory or conceptualised work that was needed. My trusting and life trained me, and those who came and still come to me are my teachers. How beautiful is that? How amazing are they?

No wonder I am in awe of our nature and cannot buy into human weakness but see mostly the strength of the human spirit.

I see the whole "veil " is simply that we have bought into the unkind lie that we are not enough and not to be trusted, which is saying we are not Divine and Creators of all that we experience.

There were times when I scared myself at the things I said to people. Like telling someone to "grow up, take their life in hand, rather than play poor me, and to go away.

Of course I doubted often, and I still look to be aware of my ego, it is part of being HUman.

Truly being with others is mostly doing and being together in that moment and not preconceiving what you are going to do with them, how you want the experience to go, or preempting the reaction or the outcome for you or the other.

You mind your own business and let them mind their own. Thus when they have gone from your presence there is no deep postmortem. Just trust, knowing love and an expanded feeling of joy for the honour of knowing them.

What I am saying is if you Love and are open and trust yourself and trust that the other person will show you what they need to be reflected back to them, then there is absolutely no reason to be afraid of what you might say to anyone. You will always do the right thing by them even if they get peeved, slam the door in your face, break down and cry their heart out, or get up and hug you and fall in love with you.

The power of love works miracles even if a person goes away and you never see them again.

I have seen time and again the result of these miracles of transformation through self-empowerment even if it is 20-30 years later. Love is never ever wasted. It is the Truth and the proof of free energy.

You are Love Incarnate and so you can do anything. If you really know the power in your own freedom then that is what you can gift others by your mere Presence. The knowing and the loving are the expanding energy that calls to its likeness in the field of another.

There is no longer any need to be afraid of ego if you befriend it.

The ego is a most beautiful safeguard and keeps us awake to our own process at all times.

CHAPTER 9

A Myth Buster

There never was a Universal Cosmic Law of Karma of "return to sender whatever was given". This was a Collective construction of humankind. An unkind lie that seemed to explain the variability of life situations and satisfy the need for fair play and justice.

The so called "fall" of humanity came from the placement of ego above and outside Divinity and Source connectedness. And in doing so, self-aware consciousness got buried in density, individuality and separateness.

Human consciousnesses (The Collective) hid themselves deeper and deeper in isolation, and the fear and hurt of that separation. Of feeling totally unsafe.

However, each and every one who reads this is a point of light within the Mind of God. You are Divine and Angelic. Through the Grace of Mother/Father/One you have been given free Will to explore and experience whatever you like in the Infinity of All Creation.

Thus for whatever reason and purpose, you have chosen every occasion you wanted to incarnate, OR NOT, at any time. You were never forced to do any of it by some Divine Law.

And each time you stepped out of your body you would assimilate your experiences into your Knowing and remembering, into the Pure Golden Light that YOU ARE as Soul Being.

You never came back into a 3D Earth life for self-punishment at any time and there are so many reasons why any one of you would return, but frequently it would be to fine tune your Knowing of a particular density experience and unlovingness.

In this incarnation, besides individual Soul Choice, WE have all come to experience the joy and wonder of the transformation of our body field into LIGHT and to participate in the undoing of all the "unkind lies" that were ever told to Humans. Not just to you personally but also to the ancestral memories you carry within the DNA of your present body vehicle.

To live a HUman life as was intended in the first place and that WE have all dreamt of.

You the Angelic Divine Being, Loving who you are, standing in Warrior strength of your own Truth of Knowing and the magnificence of the Eternal Spirit of who and what you are.

This is why HUmans are here in the first place. To experience and extract True Love in "dense" form. Isn't this what you have always searched for. Don't you see that same searching and longing of every Precious Soul you meet regardless of how they are playing their final act?

PS: And if you can continually step back and take this 10,000 ft view of your Life and who you ARE, this view from the mountain top down to the beautiful valley below and out to the great horizon, then you will not get so caught up in the moment by moment playing out of the "undoing" of old patterns that you are presently enacting. Each time you will be pressing the RESTART button.

CHAPTER 10

Going Beyond the Shared Human Trauma

The World generally and the USA in particular have dreamed of being the "Greatest" compared to everyone else and taught its children that they could be and to strive to be.

And now there is a 101 "oppositions".

How else could it be?

The old is rising because it is leaving. All the manmade divisions and mind filters are being exposed to fall away. They are leaving.

Contrast through opposition is the way the old Collective viewed things. It was required in order that we experienced all the possibilities through dramas and traumas we chose to experience in the 3rd density.

There is no energetic to support any of it any longer. All the "Loops" of miscreation are being exposed in yourselves and the international in the "out there Movie". To be erased., including the loop of so called "karmic debt".

Left versus Right.

So here it is for all to see. A kind of "sick joke" the Collective Heart of humanity has put before you in order that you make a moment to moment CHOICE to be either this or that, or neither. To no longer take sides.

Now it is about detecting the more subtle contrasts. Your own subtle deeper and personal Knowings of where you wish to move and how you wish to take your own Power. How openly you can see and acknowledge the Shadows that have been in your own field all along and have been rampant in the Human psyche.

To look beyond the traumatising contrast and see the inner beauty beneath, within and above and beyond.

Are you going to listen to your Knowing and prepared to make daily choices to step back into a New Life Stream that you are creating. Or are you still enjoying the gross contrast of the now defuncted nightmare dream sequence.

Are you willing to erase all the loops of slavery you have carried for yourself and all humanity.

Entirely up to YOU. There is no judgement here just a Profound Love that is calling you from WITHIN to make your "REAL" choices. A calling that is coming, not just from Soul Being but from all the countless layers of Light Beings in your Support Teams.

You need only talk to them through your Feelings and be prepared to ask for their mentorship, being prepared to follow the ensuing dialogue in deeper, more subtle FEELINGS.

CHAPTER 11

You are the Gift You bring to the World

There is absolutely nothing or no one out there who wants to bring you down. To teach you a lesson, to find your faults. Oh no.

In fact the reverse is your Truth. Everything, but everything, put in front of you is conspiring to bring you your highest, clearest, brightest reflection and experience of who you really are.

Do you get it? You are the Creator, the Inviter, the Director, Producer, the Actor and Audience of it all. You are the GIVER. You are the RECEIVER. And You are the GIFT.

You are the Presence. You are the Presenter. And You are the PRESENT.

It is really time to now totally TRUST yourself.

Drop all the old mental mind Loops. Step into the Flow bravely, and watch everything fit perfectly together in every way possible. Nothing will be left out.

Congratulations, welcome Home.

PS: Count on your Smile, your Shine, the Christed Light that is of your core Heart (the Divinity of SELF). Its Light touches everyone whether you see the results or not.

Perhaps this is the major reason we are here. Not to change others but to simply, honestly and Lovingly experience More

YOU as WE, and to see how the magic of Shine brings life and connects everything as ONE.

HUmaniy is Rising. Believe in yourself dear reader.
.

CHAPTER 12

The Unravelling of Collective Programmes

Nothing essential is broken.

There is nothing more to fix.

The Great tangled mess that was the dense realms of human thought creation is unravelling by itself. There is no more energy to support it.

And how did this unravelling come about?

Because you are now beginning to truly Love Yourself and in so doing you are Loving it all back into the Majestic Divine Place it has always been.

You came here to unravel the density of human thought creation through experiencing your own version of it and Now Loving it Free.

Do you get it!

Take nothing personally anymore.

CHAPTER 13

The Healing of Humanity

You see chaos in world events, and confusion and dramatic reactions in your communities and families. And you may ask "Where is the Love?"

But I tell you that I visit daily and there are people in every village, town and city in every place on Earth who know, and who daily hold the space of pure Love and compassion for all.

The pressure of the ages is upon Humanity to finally, once and for all, clear the shadows of the illusion and regain their freedom, Truth and Lovingness.

Thus all that is not of honesty and love rises. All Shadow is being exposed, out of the subconsciousness of every single person on this planet.

And you and I are here to Hold the Space of Love in our Hearts. To run the shadows through our consciousness and to Choose Light.

To clear our space in life, as we find it, and envisage, imagine, and dream the New Golden Age into manifestation.

We are cocreating through alignment with our Soul Being (higher selves) and the vast Soul and multidimensional Spirit Company.

The transformation is assured and it is this Love/Light that We ARE that is the very reason that all the dross has to come to the surface. And our Love is beyond all the boundaries and conventions of human division.

So I share with you this Message I received from a Beloved Sister from the Middle East.

I ask you that, when you have read this, to sit with her in your Heart and connect to the Love Space she holds, and many others who are doing the same in their own private connection to the Quantum Field and the WWW of LOVE. You are making a difference. Thankyou, thankyou.

"I live in Israel, and would not like to provoke any kind of emotion around the subject in an open message. I want to tell you how much your words find an echo in my heart in those moments of profound cleansing of a karmic dance of death between two members of the same family. I realise more and more that in the emotional detachment in which I observe that somehow little miracles happen every day since the beginning of the wars. As if Israel, Syria, Turkey, Lebanon, USA, or anywhere else is like the beating heart of the world leaving no one indifferent.

This world sorrow somehow brings people together, to pray or help one another. Your daily messages are strengthening this strange silence in my heart and I am grateful to realise that the awakening of consciousness is happening at all levels of our community too, in a timeline where war is one extreme, peace is the other side and still the same energy, so silence and compassion is what I try and communicate to my surroundings hoping those waves will eventually transform this chaos in a new realisation of how to build this broken family back into a loving one Thank you for being there and being here. Yes, yes We Are the Family of One. I So Love You All".

Join your Heart with Hers and Know beyond all doubt.

Your Love and willingness to live courageously in the Truth of your Knowing is making a Difference.

Love Fearlessly.

PS: And I repeat that you can walk the streets of anywhere in the world and touch with your love.

In your imagining you actually jump into another dimension and your love can touch there just as much as you can touch with someone standing right in front of you. The veils have lifted and Your Love is that powerful.

CHAPTER 14

Deepen You Relationship with Gaia

Be gentle, patient and kind to yourself. Otherwise how can you fully be gentle, patient and kind with others?

If you can you will lose your need to battle with the conditions around you.

Make friends with the 3rd dimension.

We are not leaving physicality. We are transforming in it and raising Life expressed in 3D up.

Gaia is transforming it and we are star visitors who have come here to participate as Her guests and co-contributors and creators. We are here to experience the Divinity (Higher Light) of SELF in density.

Gaia is already ascending, spinning in the 5th dimension. Thus as you reach down into Her core and connect your core through your opening Heart, She is participating in your "lifting up" into the higher dimensions of expression, transfiguring density.

Staying close to Gaia deepening your feelings and relationship with Her, and all realms, is essential in your own ascension process because the ascension is not just about you or humanity.

It is about Gaia and the whole planetary, and Solar System consciousness in physicality.

If you are not connected and anchored into Gaia and yourself you cannot hold your connection with your Heart in physicality. And if you are not connected to your Heart expression of your "God" nature and awareness you are "lagging behind" in your Joy of living and experiencing the imbalances in and around you in all the forms you can create it to be.

You are free when you can make friends with 3D and know without doubt your Beloved "God connection" (or however you wish to name it). And thus, you will experience your expansion, your awareness of everything in your Reach.

After all why did you choose to come here and now in the first place? You came to lose and rediscover your Lovingness in the densest of frequencies.

What an amazingly awesome and perfect experience it can be.

Now it is time to take yourself back and to PLAY, to giggle to laugh, in this final act of giving back the joy of your knowing to all Creation.

Shine On you funny, ridiculously seriously Precious HUman.

CHAPTER 15

Living with Frequency Focus

Life is all about frequency and what we are all engaged with at this time is becoming conscious of frequency, learning to Master it within ourselves. Becoming aware of more and more subtle feelings in our Body and Auric Field.

Realising that what is "out there" are events generated by frequencies held "within". That there is an intimate relationship between Field and Form, between within and without, between higher and lower.

When we change the frequency within we change the events without, their effect on us, and their occurrence. Frequencies that are lower and higher, of the old (Shadow) and of the new (Light).

We are getting use to feeling the waves of energy that are typical of our human experience now, in such a way that we no longer separate the troughs and the crests as "bad" and "good". In other words we drop the stories, the attachments to memories and identities.

Then we are naturally able, without fanfare, to "neutralize" and raise the "lower" frequencies and blend them with the "higher", the frequencies of Heart.

So realise that low vibration and heavy feeling isn't your fault.

You may not even know it is there or remember how you picked it up. You don't have to know what the resistance is, and you don't have to work at it, analyze it, process it, or suffer. You just feel the feeling, do your small part in allowing it to move through your body and thoughts, as emotion (energy in motion). You Love, and Grace does the rest.

You simply feel and allow and your Being, your Divine Presence does the other 90% through Grace.

Just open up to it.

Enlightenment is simply being in the natural Divine Golden Flow of who You are. Shadow fades away in the Light of your higher (Divine) Knowing, and with this Knowing you replace the now vacant "space" with your Lovingness.

You remove lower Light frequency by creating a vacuum into which higher Light frequency can be streamed.

When you no longer try to fix anything, and just let go, Grace puts you back in that Flow, and does most of the work (with the help of your Divine Support Team). It naturally, effortlessly paves the way to abundance for you and for those around you whom you touch.

Shine On

PS: And at another level, you can accelerate this process by developing a closer, deeper, more intimate cocreative relationship with your Divine Team (and a specific "higher" guide mentor) who has access to information in your Soul Being (with your freewill permission) that you do not have access to (conscious knowledge of) while in embodiment.

Chaper 16 The Divine Mystery Revealed Perhaps?

Do you want to find more of you? Then let me tell you the secret of the ages.

It has been Known by true mystics in all traditions and cultures. It cannot be spoken of nor described. But it is available to you and has always been there residing within you.

I can point to it and only you can discover the reality of IT.

Put aside for a moment all religion, spiritual description all New Age "gobble de gook", channeled messages from on "high". And everything I have written here.

It is so, so SIMPLE.

If you would Know God. Know SELF, Know the "Peace that Passeth all Understanding". Then listen, watch, and feel.

There is a Song of Creation that plays Eternally within you. You will hear it as a constant ringing within and without………Listen.

There is a Light that Shines within you (with eyes closed and eyes open). Though it may be faint at first the more you watch the brighter it becomes………Watch.

There is a soft and strong, ever so subtle subliminal Presence (beyond any naming of it) within you constantly……….Feel it.

And Beloved HUman Being, Brother/Sister of my Heart.

It all depends on Trusting Silence.

And Smiling because it has to been whispered to you and you have Heard.

PS: And some who read this will skip it putting no significance on it whatsoever.

And some will puzzle over it and go back to ornate descriptions of Truth and seek more to fill the void.

And some will recognize and perhaps explore further experiences of pure SELF.

And some of you will get the Awesome Beauty and Profundity of this 'practice" of "The Way" that is being pointed to.

And there is absolutely no judgement here Precious Souls.

YOU are LOVE and YOU are LOVED

Beyond...... Beyond.

CHAPTER 17

Ego Points the Way

A message from a friend.

"I've thrown away totally my ego, it is a thing of the past and life has been awesome since. However, in my dreams, whilst asleep the ego is still within my character? Is this a message or do I have to work much harder during meditation to rid the ego entirely ?"

You cannot rid yourself of ego. It is a Divine seed you have allowed to be planted in your consciousness in order to negotiate this densest reality, having been given free will.

It is there to constantly remind you when you feel disconnected from Source.

It is a beautiful aspect of your expression, as you are in human form, that gives you a sense of individuality.

It reminds you when you separate yourself and isolate yourself from that which is within and around you, that which You ARE, Eternally.

How would you have known that there was something other than what you were experiencing when you were travelling in darkness?

Your ego has been ever pressing you into the experience of separation in order for you to wake up. To seek for something else, to make connection to All That Is.

So you see, my dear friend, that it has been your lifeline and is most beloved. And when it arises, give thanks that it is there to immediately point the way, when you are not where you feel most "at Home".

And you see how clever you are because in your dream you have played out the separation you are making and the ego is asking you to acknowledge it as an aspect of you that tells you when you are not on song, "in the zone".

As long as you are in HUman form and Soul Being, you will have Ego. You will just become quicker and quicker at recognising when you are there in disconnection by its presence, until you are able to step back into your Truth Knowing in a flash.

And because you know what being "in ego" is, you will have the connection, through that Knowing to the understanding, and the Compassion for every other Being that is identifying with their "ego" and feeling disconnected.

Be afraid no more of this beloved seed truth marker in you.

PS: There is an inflow and an outflow. This is the way of creation.

There is moving from center outwards in all directions, like an expanding circle, and there is an inflow from all directions spiraling up back to center.

And when you are in outflow there are an infinite number of points or places you can be conscious of in that circle of outpouring. When you walk in that world you experience from a single point. It is your point of viewing. It is a "place you have chosen to view from. And it is ego that allows you to stop for a moment to take in the view.

But when you begin to take that view as "the" reality, as all there is then you get "stuck". You become fixed because you are identifying with that reality, YOU, as being the only point of view. This is your ego in operation and it allows you to "apparently" stay in the one place for as long as you wish to be there. We are what we identify with.

When you meditate or are centered, or choose your Lovingness, you are in Heart. The Infinite Stillness of Being in its inflow and Infinite Embrace of Love in its outflow.

As a HUman being the ego seed is still present but dormant. It is only when you take a point of view, and identify with it as being YOU, that you are "in ego". And it is this sense of a singular point of view, this ego state, that reminds you that you are stuck or over identifying with where you are or "what you are all about".

Simply STEP BACK to your Heart even for a moment and the "point of viewing" changes.

IT (YOU) Expand.

Ego fades and rests easy.

CHAPTER 18

Meditate, Meditate, Meditate

By "meditate" I point to you being with and in YOURSELF, in Heart, without and beyond thought.

Find your place of Quietness and Stillness.

Yes, Yes…….. I know it is elusive but through loving perseverance You WILL cross into the Great FLOW of SELF.

It is not something only for a monk or someone who has sequestered themselves "away from" everyday Life. It is natural for some to spend hours in this place while for others only a brief step back into it is necessary. There is not "better"or lesser". Each serves the all with what comes naturally and joyously for them.

However, any such practice, in fact, will enhance everything you experience in life as you find it.

And because of the pull of your version of the 'matrix', it requires that you do it daily.

I 'die' daily (let go of my HUman identity) into the God/Source Presence I AM.

And you will find this immersion seeps more and more into your day until you can 'slip' into it at will.

You will so Love how it feels that it will become Presence of Being.

PS: A major theme running through this book, points you here.

I encourage, cajol, prod, and celebrate you to take to this daily dive into SELF.

If you want to make this ascension journey with more Grace and ease and less frustration and feeling "stuck" then being with yourself beyond mental mind (and that infernal mind chatter) is required. It is possible. It is do-able. I have been doing it and teaching it for 50 years.

How much would you like this. How committed are you to find this inner Peace that is beyond all understanding?

PPS: Just saying.

You have all this extra time. It is called by human "lockdown", but could it really have been a gift to you to taste more time in SOUL PRESENCE??

"Social distancing", as more freedom from the disturbances of the auric presence of others ?

"Masks", as an opportunity to practice Smile with your eyes.

"Isolation", as an more freedom from distraction and opportunities to choose Light On.

CHAPTER 19

On Being Bold.

Many have all the "right" ideas, the "right" knowing, the "right" things to say, and yet still hide the Light of their Soul.

Isn't it about time you "came out".

To be Bold is not about putting yourself out there, and pushing yourself onto others. It is about bringing forward your courage to be who you are. The courage to follow your intuition, your heart prompts, your inner knowing, ALL THE TIME.

And don't tell me you are not getting inner prompts moment to moment. That you are not being guided, cajoled, and pushed as to what is right for you to do at any moment you care to stop and listen.

Are you prepared to follow without excuse, or the need to know where it will lead, and with a total trust in yourself and how the Universe brings everything that will fulfil you to your "table", in magnificent timing and surprise?

Are you bold enough to receive all the amazing "goodies" that can be presented to you?

And when you have listened enough, discovered the beauty of this dance of You, you will be able to walk into the market place and boldly, confidently say "hello to the world".

You will greet it with a smile and feel the freedom to go up and speak to anyone if you get the slightest prod to do so. You will not be thinking at all of how you might appear.

Your nature is to be pleasant, kind, and offer your touch of Love freely to anyone, unabashed, for you know your

Lovingness and can only see the beauty in the other person. You know the Universe is totally benevolent and thus you trust that your gift to another will be received by the truth of that person.

You hear a call from another for the Touch of Love and that is what you do. You are a Master and where is the mastery but in the Freedom of Self being consciousness? To walk unabashed in the world is Mastery. And it is an unkind excuse to say that you do not want to be 'arrogant.

Don't you know that true confidence and humility go together?

Stop "being selfish" share your joy with the world.

As you feel the world let the world feel You.

Shine On.

CHAPTER 20

The Great Shining is Here

You have come such a long way. You are here and you need no longer fear that you could ever go back. You have mastered the worlds of darkness. Loving it to total inclusion, into inclusion as the side that Light had not been. And you have left your mark of light wherever you have gone.

You are becoming fully at Home with yourself here, aligning fully with Gaia, and now it is only a matter of believing this totally, and living exactly how you feel it. How your self-honesty reveals your way to more You, moment by moment.

Breathe it all in as you anchor your fullness with Earth in your body and Knowing, and in that infinitesimal moment between breath sequence, you are One in Source. In the letting go of all limitation, the out breath becomes an expansion of Love, your loving embrace as a flow in your Being through doing.

PS: And remember that it has been a terrible, unkind lie of propaganda for you to be afraid of Father Sun. The Life Giving, Life Promoting waves of Cosmic Light stream through Him bathing and transmuting us All.

And in His present outpouring you will have noticed how His Flares of Fire and Transmutation, like a Dragons Breath, brings waves and days of bodily weakness and the need to rest and sleep. Then afterwards days of vitality and aliveness, clarity, alignment and wellbeing.

And in Joy this will not lessen but is accelerating. So simply Flow with it.

You asked for transformation and it is happening for Everyone. There is no hiding anymore. It is time to fully surrender to this natural evolutionary process, and you will become more acclimatised to it.

So bless and honour Father Sun, and go visit Him. Stand in His Fire for a brief moment and allow Him to shoot you into the worlds, waves, timelines, and Love through and beyond your present knowing.

CHAPTER 21

You are Living on the Cutting Edge: JUMP

To All those Standing on the Edge, ready to jump, to Fly Free and to Live your Purpose, your Shine, in total surrender to SELF, even though you do not know clearly what your purpose is exactly.

We are not alone and never have been, though we have chosen to experience the feelings of being disconnected from everything.

Now, in our grand awakening we see that, not only are we connected to everything, but that our individual purpose will be expressed and fully realised in our connectedness to all things.

And dear reader, it is my experience that gaining the real confidence in myself comes from the trust to make the leaps into the unknown.

I do not know how you will react to what I am writing but I have developed the confidence to follow my prompts. I trust me, but also I trust you. I trust that however you react that you have the capacity to handle it from your point of view.

So the leap is in reality, not trying to work the consequences all out. Not trying to box it up through control, which is fear based. Not trying to preempt anything. Not concerning myself with what you may think because I know my own lovingness and that it is the expressing of it that makes my reality Whole and complete in any given moment.

Trusting, acting, and allowing that the Universe, Creation, is totally unbiased and allows for the possibility for the most benevolent outcome for All of us.

Trust your heart knowing and act upon it all ways.

And I receive so many beautiful gifts of loving from others and the Universe throughout my days. I have stopped looking for the gifts to come but through my experience of trusting, acting and letting go, I get these gems from everywhere.

And so to give, and to give, and to give, and while giving I am forever open to receive. And So it Is Done, continually.

Thus jump dear Sister or Brother, jump. And expect and know that, apart from gaining more experience of the Master that you are, you will experience little and big priceless miracles.

"You ain't seen nothing yet".

And your going to see a lot of us flying around with you.

Jump.

CHAPTER 22

Living from a 5th Dimensional State

Someone wrote to me:

"I have always tried to work out all details prior to an experience or before it happens-to the point of depriving myself of sleep. How silly! Things never work out that way, and just to be able to relax and let things "happen", wow, what freedom."

To All who know what she is moving into because you are experiencing it now.

You chose your own destiny aeons ago so you cannot avoid it otherwise you would not experience the knowing you came for.

Absolutely NO harm can come to you. You have chosen to move into your Beingness of total unconditional Love which is here and NOW (Gaia has already moved Herself and been making Her alignments for ages).

From 5D you beginning to fully realise that there is no "death", so you drop that fear for yourself for a start.

And do not fear for others for they are making their choices, their own Soul and Being Knows.

You become willing to claim, that everything is conspiring to bring you the fullest Knowing of your Lovingness, while the remnants of the old 3D human systems plays itself out.

Just as you cannot fit yourself or your life into a "box" anymore, the energies of your expansion do not allow it, so too the rules and constructions of the old human system don't work anymore. They are collapsing in all our government, finance, medical, legal, educational, systems. And any attempts to patch them up are doomed to failure. The higher frequencies of Self (5D+ energies, if you will) just do not support them.

And your Love helps it all on its way out.

And as you feel your freedom. you live more from 5D but reaching down into 3D at the highest frequency, transmuting your body/Being and everything you touch.

And as 3D human structures are collapsing there are people all around the world quietly, steadily working with new creative solutions that are aligned with the Unconditional energies of Love, Freedom, and Unity.

And your Shine affects everyone you see and who feels it.

And everyone of you who reads this has chosen Love and has an entourage of Spirit Family with you. Angels, guides, Masters and Star Family, faeries, little folk behind you cheering you on, waiting for your requests for healing, knowledge and help to move through new doorways and portals of your Remembering and Experiencing.

Please don't forget to ask and to talk to them, and step beyond all your doubts into the multidimensional access now available to you. if you would simply step towards it within you.

Ask for constant reminders for the removal of all your doubts. Go to the inner healing chambers and/or the Starships awaiting your call. Watch all aches, pains and ailments and even genetic and long term blockages pass through you without fear and with empowered thoughts of your Loving connection to All That Is.

Develop your love filled relationships with all Creation.

There is Nothing else Left To Fear.

LOVE is here to stay.

CHAPTER 23

Creating Your New Earth Experience

Through our rational mind training we have all developed a kind of "knee jerk" scepticism where your mind reacts immediately to new things, or things we are unfamiliar with, or have little or no memory of having experienced.

It is at the basis of all our doubts about ourselves. It says that "this is not possible in my reality".

However, in order to move, to grow, you are being required to step beyond yourself.

So contemplate this deeply.

If anything appears to you as being impossible then know it IS POSSIBLE. For this, and your courage to leap into it, into the unknown of it, maybe your next shift into your freedom, into your enlightenment.

The magic of Life is in your valuing of it.

Remember your enchantment in the magic of fairy tales and "make believe" when you were young.

As for your doubts, first you learn to ignore and step back from them. Then, seeing the doubts pop up, you choose to smile and say "no thankyou". You take your own Knowing in the first 3 seconds of its appearance and begin consciously choosing the thoughts and feelings that reflect the deep core of myths, and mysteries as a young child.

Then reclaim it now. Return to the power of PRE-TEND.

You are well and truly alive in the 4th Dimension. The dimension in which you can create Your Dream and begin to Live in it. It starts to becomes a LUCID dream in your waking state. It is the precursor to it manifesting in the 3rd dimension from the unconditional Love dimension (5th if you will) if you choose.

Be fascinated, delighted and enthralled by the reality you are at present experiencing, by the gifts of others, their courage and their interests, and you will positively love what is to come.

Cultivate consciously and deliberately your sensed of Reverence, Awe, and Wonder about the All that is possible "out there".

What do you want to Create for your New Earth Dream.

Your creations will emerge from your feeling now.

Feeling, Joy, Curiosity, a sense of adventure, a revelling in the new, a sense of awe and wonder, a love of the new, the delight of sharing in simple pleasures, and the excitement of the unexpected, in these Now moment is leading you through The Golden Doorway into our New Life on Nova Gaia.

Be reverent and resolute in your choice to Dream Big and live in such a way that your create the feelings.

This IS NOT avoiding life as it is.

It is called "Being Truly ALIVE"..

PS: And my beautiful friend "the littlest fairy" comes to sit on my shoulder. And she says

"Tell them we are here". Tell them that love is in the tiniest and the greatest. It is within them and around and through them. Tell the dear hearts to stop, look, and listen and they will see and feel love and the magic everywhere. It has always been hidden in plain view. Even the noisy cities and towns are no longer any boundary to its all pervading reach and touch.

Tell them that they came here to create from their own most magnificent Dream"

CHAPTER 24

Moving from Logic to Feeling.

Reminding you to stop letting your mind interpret everything or anything before you feel it.

"In the Flow" means coming from Heart Knowing and this is a Knowing in Feeling.

Whenever you find yourself processing in mind, trying to find and fix the meaning of anything through analysis, then mostly you are in fear (doubt) ,and "Spiritual" versions of your story are still dramas until you no longer identify them as being a mark of who you are.

It is now all about flow, following your heart, opening to new, gaining the real experience that it is in this internal, eternal knowing, that life reveals itself in its pristine spirit and form.

Your Shift is about consciously raising and loving in higher frequency and we do this NOW. We do it by choosing Love and living in the joyful experience of it.

And when we are not, it is simply a matter of feeling where the fear is, gently acknowledging it, and choosing heart, and watching the fear shift and move and leave without a story.

And from this choice we can then use mind to form the reality we wish to create in that moment, rather than use it to go over why all your past happened, and develop another box to put it in because we have recreated it.

Only then can you construct (play) with the mental mind, but the construction will now be based on higher frequency thought in feelings, seasoned always with your knowing of Love and the experience of Joy (the inner Smile).

"Stay the course"

Choose your Shine for every step you can.

PS: Haven't you noticed that things are happening so fast you cannot prepare for them? Doesn't this tell you something?

Perhaps you are already prepared for it and now you are being shown that you need not doubt it any longer because everything is working, It is all OK, and you can cruise, float and soar in amongst it all. It all works and is working out, so there is NOTHING MORE that has to be Fixed.

Stop defining and classifying just "get over it".

Place your right hand where it will naturally go to the middle of your chest above your heart. Now just breath it, feel it. Feel what happens and be open to it. You can do this anytime, anywhere, and the feeling, the knowing of this Lovingness expands. It is in you, around you. It IS You.

No words of labelling, just a glowing, flowing, growing You.

So if you would know your Higher Heart", the Love That You Are. begin here in any given moment.

CHAPTER 25

Cutting the Cords to Old Ways of Thinking.

Why do you think you have experienced your "trials and traumas"?

You have been transforming the human "suffering" and victimhood, into Love and Compassion for it all.

It was not yours in the first place but you agreed to do it.

You agreed to bring your own version of a piece of this "matrix". To experience it as yours and then step out of it, by Remembering who you are and bringing your Love to bare on Yourself and all that had passed "through" you.

And in this "clearing" of yourself you have cleared a piece for the whole planet and all time.

In the realisation that none of it was yours, you now know that you do not need fixing and never have.

You were on a trajectory that brings you to this point that has enabled you to complete this part of your Lifestream.

And this is how Magnificent You ARE.

You cut all cords to the old ways of viewing the physical reality. No more descending into loops of the "nightmare dream sequence".

You are here now bringing the codings and information contained in photonic light, through your physical body, thus enlivening and opening DNA strings of every cell in your body. Activating your Divine Body Blueprint.

You are here to Love, to play, create, expand and Shine the LIGHT that You Are.

YOU ARE the GIFT for others to align with the truth of their own trajectory.

PS: Each of us adds the unique Gift that WE ARE to the Collective, and makes available an increasing and ever amplifying potential choice for others to move more quickly on their own Divine trajectory.

You are not here to fix yourself or others. You were never broken.

BE also aware.

That your gift is not the in the suffering. That was optional Your freewill choices. It is in the Remembering and Loving.

CHAPTER 26

End Game: The Real Conspiracy - (Part I)

I am not one for Conspiracy Theories but here is one that would be worth your while to entertain. We have come here across the Cosmos as System Busters. Adults in the awakening, teens in rebellious turmoil, and children in the knowing.

Come to choose and see Love each in our unique expression and perfect placement (assignment).

"Hand (Heart) picked" this moment. You have come as a Living breathing physical conduit for your Lovingness. Infiltrators in every walk of life, Shining the photon Light, enlivening and calling it out in everyone in your vicinity.

Secret agents fulfilling your mission on a "need to know" basis. Which means that you do not know what you are going to do next and you may not see the effect, but it is part of a Great Plan, the Divine Source's Plan, for the liberation of HUman Consciousness and the Creating of a Golden Age on Nova Gaia.

And no person, Being or Master knows exactly how it will unfold. You just know that the blueprint is written indelibly in your cellular nature and in your Heart.

A Divine secret that cannot be voiced but is known deep within you. You are here to experience the unfolding of The Master You ARE, through the experience and embrace of all that your days bring to you.

YOU are a unique piece of the Great Master Plan.

It is a Divine Opportunity that you were overjoyed to participate in. It is not an experience nor just a service that you are giving and then going back "Home" as soon as you can.

The success of the Mission requires us all to live and play together in acceptance and harmony, and the completion is Inevitable.

The invincible weapon of the Armageddon is of course, you guessed it, The Universal, Unconditional LOVE each one of us carry.

And the fuse is set (or the Bow is drawn).

Aim straight and TRUE Warriors, every one.

PS: You have experienced 3D and in your REMEMBERING, everything you have Known is turned on its head. Knowing only the Present of who you ARE and what you are Eternally Unified with, and firmly grounded on Gaia you aim True without seeing a singular target.

Your Heart Knows where to aim

Strong and steadfast and in complete Knowing (Faith) you........ Let GO.

CHAPTER 27

End Game Part II: Weapons of Mass Distraction

Fear has been a massive marketing tactic for Humanity.

Of course this Shift in the Consciousness of All can be rough, weird, and wonderful at times. But dear Friends find your calmness and learn to be able to go there at will through this time of chaos for so many.

Change is now the NORMAL. Earth changes, celestial events, ET interaction, vivid dreams, visions, unexplainable perception and sensations, aches and pains of all kinds are the NORMAL.

The burning fire of the incineration of lower level egoic, emotional and thought forms are NORMAL. The sudden outburst of emotional feeling is NORMAL. The rising of mental mind confusion, and blankness (loss of short term memory) is NORMAL. The rise of the kundalini and the opening of the pineal gland (lifting of the veils) is NORMAL. The massive and increasing infusion of photonic Light in the very cells of your body is NORMAL.

The unusual aspect of this particular Shift is that it is the Ascension of the whole HUman Collective to a new higher expression of Planetary Consciousness.

You cannot learn to activate Source Light in programs designed to disempower and distract.

Conspiracy and other nonsense are old programs designed to restrict HUman ascension. Some may have started with good intentions to wake people up, but they forget to evolve above the old paradigm.

The gap between intent/focus/thought and manifestation in your personal life has to disappear, thus disconnecting from any remaining emotional attachments to negative programs is essential.

And I am not suggesting that you go bury your head in the sand, retreat from the world, and ignore what appear to be "out there". On the contrary it requires you to be fully grounded and Present 24/7.

Be aware there is still the lure to use suffering to fall back on when change feels scary. Conspiracy programs can cleverly convince you to create realities which do not exist anymore. They teach you how to create a barrier between you and the truth, energetic enslavement of your expression being fed by low-vibrational thought forms (shadow beings), and emotional triggers.

Even the deliberate attempts to make people suffer is designed to pull you into pity and sadness and take you away from your well earned deep Compassionate Knowing.

These are OLD programs, which do not serve the New Light within you, and it means that a whole lot of folks are missing out on the truth of ascension as yet. Unfortunate, since people are often convinced they are finding the truth through these programs.

Interestingly, even though the energies which built and sustained these old programs has gone since 12/12/2012, personal attachment to the mental and emotional habitual loops of humans continue to recreate or maintain them.

The distractions are numerous, subtle and outright devious at times, often fired by any subconscious lie you might not have faced up to that you are still holding.

As the old crumbles it can become very difficult for those without heart-center coherence to decipher what is true, what is illusion, and what is absolutely aimed at inhibiting their own evolution.

Discernment requires that you always take your highest perspective before you react.

These New Light Waves are not out to get you, nor are the old structures and systems. Anyone still focusing on the Shift as some kind of biblical or 'karmic', destructive tool aimed at crushing the dark is way off beam, and the same goes for the frustrating and disempowering stance of waiting for the collapse.

You ARE the Shift. The responsibility for change rests with you.

The Shift is Planetary as well as HUman, and Gaia has already made Her Shift while the density time-lag is disappearing rapidly.

So all this is asking "what are you doing Right Now?"

How are you applying your power of instant manifestation of positive, heart-based thought, as well as instant release of the manifestation of subconscious baggage of the old operating systems.

Take your Mask off.

What are you creating under there?

You are So Loved.

PS: As long as you can be drawn into self-doubt the "matrix " is still operative in your Field. How might you clear it?

Call in your Spirit support (angels or Soul Mentor Guides, etc.) who are Always present with and around you.

Relax and ask "Please go into my Field and pluck out the shadow that is activating this self doubt (specify it especially about the feeling it gives you).

Just know that they will do this, even instantaneously. It is done. Then go back into your heart and choose any thought or tool you have to amplify any feel you love having.

And there you are back in alignment.

We all can benefit immensely to do this at least once each day, sometimes a few times.

It is part of living in this HUman Field.

I am not immune.

But we get quicker and quicker at doing it.

Relax, tune in to your Team (who are always available) and ask. IT IS DONE.

How beautiful is THAT?

CHAPTER 28

From Sacred Heart: A Field of Flowers

As you imagine and view from your heart and expand and see the beautiful blue Earth below/within you, can you see all the lights?

As you look closer can you see the glowing flower lights rising?

The rising of HUmanity.

Can you see the man in overalls with greasy hands working to bring enough home to feed his family day after day?

Can you see the women on her knees scrubbing, the office worker pouring over papers on their desk, the student sitting in a library, your neighbours going to the same work day after day?

Can you see the slavery and the bravery?

Can you see the desperateness and the hope?

Can you see the confusion and the moments of insight and happiness?

Can you see the larger plan, each Precious Soul in their Divine Knowing having the great courage to take this journey of forgetting and experiences of compassion from every angle possible in this dual density?

Do you feel the honour and privilege to see them, to know them, to be connected to them?

Does your heart swell with Love, with the knowing that this is all coming to an end as we learn to Truly Share our Lovingness fully and completely without conditions?

Do you see them rising and "Heaven" descending?

Do you see the Golden Light permeating every Heart, body and field of Being?

Can you stand amongst them feeling the peace and joy of your own rising?

Can you sing your song of Freedom through your radiating Presence?

Can you sing a song of the New Earth that is here now?

Can you let them hear and feel the truth, and let them know through your certainty that the nightmare dream sequence is over forever?

Can you give them your Truth of Being by simply being 'near' them and Shining. By being totally immune to any response, thought form, or image that is not singing in harmony with your new song?

See these flowers of HUmanity, rising and shining.

See and feel them all about you.

Watch them blossom. Every single one of them is coming Home.

Spur them on with the Radiance of your Knowing, your lovingness.

Shine On

CHAPTER 29

From Chaos to Peace

So what do you do when you see or hear of events that appear horrific, or worrisome, or bring up anger and fear, and feelings of helplessness? What do you do when you see the lies, deception, and utter desperateness of your politics, big business, the "Cabal" , etc, etc, etc.

First stop habitually exposing yourself to it.

Second take your reaction, rather than the event and say "what can I do now? How can I bring love to it? " How can I bring the Truth of who I AM to it in this moment?

Then take your knowing of the hurt and pain being experience by either the victims, or the perpetrators, or both and, in your imagination (imaging in), be with them. Let them feel your Shine your Lovingness your LIGHT embrace. And really and truly Bless them.

And to Bless them is to honour the Innocence and Truth of who you are and thus who they (WE) truly are because you have remembered that we all came into this dense reality to experience loss and lack, to contrast with our Knowing of Love and Abundance and to live the whole Amazing experience of this REMEMBERING.

You live in a quantum universe and your lovingness is more real and powerful than any event and the unlovingness that is playing itself out.

As so many of us are doing this, we put each and every "actor" of a fear based "matrix" into "containment". A containment of Light and Love (where angels and star Being gather}, and their own actions are quickly reflected back to them. They will feel the repercussions more strongly and more immediately when they act on unlovingness through the Loving Presence you are, and a mellowing begins within them and grows.

Just watch how rapidly our world is changing, how people are changing. You contribute each time you show your mastery over your own choices for the Essence of your Being, rather than your reactions to the illusion, the unkind lies.

And before you can do any of this to its fullness you have to have done THE WORK of this same on and with YOURSELF.

And it is done step by step. It is Living Your own DESTINY.
YOU ARE THE JOURNEY.
Shine On

PS: Look to the stars, the sky. And in its expansiveness, in the AWE of it all you discover the ENORMITY of YOU. Your ORIGINS and your PURPOSE.

Always with feet anchored firmly on the Ground (Mama Gaia) and fully Present in your body. Plugged IN (Earthed) and switched ON (AWARE, OPEN and ALIVE).

CHAPTER 30

Mother Love

As I breathed in the feminine energies and received and owned them more fully, I felt more and more Oneness with Mother. I notice the falling away of the "courser" elements of my "maleness" and the giving way to childlike qualities of a young and eager boy.

The Love I AM is Mother Love.

As I let go I Am in pure awareness. That watchful. ever patient, ever flowing, ever embracing of everything in Her/Our Creation.

Sweeping the floor, writing notes for my next book, smelling a flower, walking a busy street, all is perfection, all is a precious child of my/our creation. And when I forget, or when I feel annoyed, or sad, or envious, or lacking, it is fleeting and reminds me of the brilliant colours of life and how glad I am to be here now, and how awesome it is to play in so many different playgrounds and with such a amazing variety of other people (other "mees").

I no longer "need" anyone or anything and yet everyone and everything is always here and all I do is think of it, think of you, and you are here.

My prayer is my love for you All Ways.

There is no more Karma. No more serious processing to be done or any need to be "vigilant". Watching but not "on the watch".

All the bodily changes that are happening are part of a perfect unfolding of the new range of self-awareness. Just letting go of the ego's wanting to know and control.

It is enough to experience the interplay between the child who plays totally in the moment with whatever is present, and in the spaces, pure awareness and peace of the watching Mother who nurtures, supports, and loves absolutely everything in Her creation, in a flow of perfection. And the Father who holds the Power of Place.

Any remnant of the old feelings of fear, when there are symptoms that are beyond my apparent control or with no explanations, disappears in pure awareness or fades when bathed in the Eternal LIGHT/Love I AM.

These symptoms are the energies that are entering our bodies for perfect alignment and freedom. Trust, rest, ground in the Light of pure awareness of being here. They will each pass. Our body is Divine and if you love it, it will show you what it needs.

And I have discovered that because I am here in embodiment, that it is through my body feeling of alignment that I have the key to all Knowing, all Truth telling, all release of emotional, mental and spiritual discord, for all ages and times in density.

If you must, then move to some remedy or healing modality that will give your body help and comfort. However, the bottom line is that our body knows what to do if only we listen and allow.

Speak to it like a Mother would speak lovingly to a child who is finding his/her own way in the world.

May you travel Light and Free.

CHAPTER 31

Anger Management

Irritation, grumpy, anger bouts are a widespread experience in these times.

Just maybe stamping around with your anger, swearing and shouting and then coming to "No more" may be more helpful than continually trying to suppress what is naturally arising?. And this is best done out of earshot so that inadvertently another will not take it on, or you both become embroiled in another meaningless drama.

We have done more harm to ourselves by trying to bottle it and cover it with some "goody, goody two shoes" spiritual ideal and "poofery".

Doing this, getting it out, then feeling the truth of the wrath of "No more" holding back my Truth, rather than replaying the you story or events that have triggered the anger. Focusing on the bodily sensations and TRUTH Feeling of the emotion.

Then Knowing and Compassion will flow more easily for All.

It is so OK to feel what you feel.

Just learning to take it further. and see the strength and power and Love of you that lays beneath/beyond/within, will take a while to get the hang of it.

There is nothing with feeling angry. It is all about you discovering your power and a new depth of who you ARE. And it is scary to let yourself go after all this time because there have been so many judgement and fear laid upon you if you do.

And the truth about this anger is that it is not a power "over" but a power "within". And when you truly discover this you will never feel the need to manipulate, control, or 'kowtow' to another.

None of us are helpless and when we feel the sadness of being helpless then it is time to (get up off our arse), take back our power to create....to Love. That is, unless you enjoy being a miserable wretch.

The unkind lie we sucked ourselves into is that our thoughts and our emotions are not ours to have dominion over. This is utter Bullshit.........No Elephant Shit.

However, the wisdom is in the discernment of knowing what is yours and what is not. And you will never know this unless you own the energy of your own "anger" (power) feelings and learn to befriend them. Learn to take your Will, your strength, your Truth in the knowledge of the awesome power of your Lovingness and never again fall into the victimhood that says that any other has dominion over any of your Chi, your Life Force.

PS: You are NOT FLAWED because you are HUman and can 'blow a fuse". We came to experience separation. This is what 3D is about.......the experience of separateness in all things and how Love. our Lovingness, can bring it all back together because it is the Essence of who you ARE.

Your emotions are not baggage, only the stories and dramas are. They are about the energy, frequency and power of You.. Don't be "Nice" any more. Be honest, authentic, genuine, real and alive within yourself. SHINING and Sharing YOU.

CHAPTER 32

Many Hearts One Trajectory.

I often refer to standing in your own Mastery, allowing and being your own "healer". But I am not saying that if you seek help, guidance, and keys from another that somehow you are failing.

Oh no. We have chosen a collective time and a collective journey. Everyone is to have the opportunity to choose their ascension NOW.

Humanity as a whole is rising and that is why you are here. To be ready, willing and able to stand in your own light, TO BE REAL, and offer out your hand in your Shine, in the joy of you Being You.

It is an individual expression in a Collective Lucid Dream. We all came here to establish a reality, in embodiment, of the Magnificent Potential of Unity Consciousness as HUman.

A good part of our "healing" to wellbeing, and transformation is in open Loving SHARING.

This is why this and many other teachings provide a real and palpable Presence.

It is YOU here Now, as the "Family" who read and will read this book, that make this possible.

So feel your freedom, to seek a guiding heart when you feel it is right for you. Unity Consciousness is about "Holding Hands".

The efficacy of any method, modality, or teaching is in the Heart of the Giver. And thus I say it is about your discernment and resonance.

Without judging another, if your journey ultimately is deeper into your own heart then it is that which would be the best way to go to seek the Hand that can help you, no matter what the modality, or what people promise.

Trust yourself and Source even in the willingness to seek any particular guiding hand.

PS: "Healers" are at different places in their journey and can unknowingly "dump' their stuff" on to you in their "zeal to be someone". One of the criteria I see as useful is to sense the sincerity, authenticity, and simplicity of their approach, however they are doing what they do. Trust your Heart.

CHAPTER 33

The Power You have to Make a Change for All.

Beloved reader.

From time to time we all wonder just how it will be possible for the turn around of humanity to occur.

Just remember how far you have come to feel more freedom within yourself.

Waking up is not only possible for everyone, it is inevitable.

We are doing it, and I would remind you that each choice you and I make for non-judgemental loving kindness in thought, word and action, any moment, makes it so much easier for the next person to do likewise. Or thoughts and intentions are made available to all in the Quantum Field of consciousness.

As we discover ourselves and turn up our Light, it is broadcast wherever you go.

It (your Shine) touches others because their Soul Knows, their Soul recognises, their Soul has never forgotten.

WE (the millions who are dedicating their life to their awakening) have already tipped the scales and the momentum builds every second.

Every look of love, every smile, every prayer, every footstep, every kind word, every gentle touch of you, every conscious choice, becomes a Blessing.

We are doing it.

Thankyou, thankyou, thankyou.

Shine On

PS: And there is a Great Plan and Not One will be missed.

CHAPTER 34

Share Who You are with Realistically.

You do not have to be a genius to know that Humanity is HURTING. Hurting deeply, and in a state of great turmoil, fear, retrenchment, and mental and emotional crisis.

As Lightworkers We are privy and blessed to have access to Observing from the "Higher ground" of Heart Knowing if we choose.

For most this choice is not an option they can consider. They are trapped in feelings of overwhelm and the necessity to seek safety in a crumbling contrived and manipulated self-serving system. Highly influenced by the whims and agendas of those they rely on for guidance.

By and large you will not change other people's minds by arguing, long debates, or an over zealous desire to share where you are coming from.

Humanity for too long has been too dumbed down and brainwashed, through fear and lack programming to not feel threatened when the "status quo" of their beliefs are challenged. You will only increase feelings of threat and confusion, fear, and anger or withdrawal (fight or flight).

Dropping seeds (little "love bombs) of self-empowerment is far more useful. Seeds as simple questions presented simply.

Wherever you live there are always opportunities to drop 'a little something' now and again along with your Loving Touch, and then move on.

Finding a bridge between yourself and the other that they can understand, and more importantly, feel in those moments that you interact.

You let their Soul Being and their life path use the Love stimulus energy to spark off within them Light on their own journey.

We have the opportunity, and the duty to serve our Brothers and Sisters in the marketplace.

How deep and Open is Your Love?

How can YOU Love Fearlessly and stand beside anyone, even though they may hold beliefs that are "apparently" diametrically opposed to your own?

Towards the ONE.

CHAPTER 35

Toward Unity in Galactic Consciousness

Remember that the human form and expression is made up of a monumental mixture of DNA star seeds.

Look about you and you will have discovered that many people you know well are very familiar to you, and many at times seem rather strange and unfathomable (even brothers and sisters and family).

You cannot relate to them all from your mind. But they are all part of you since within you are imprints of all the starseeds.

Furthermore, you are here to gather up, within yourself, all aspects, all resonances of the Great Galactic expression deposited within Earth over the eons, and whose Light weave is embedded in your Auric Field.

So do not waste your time trying to understand everyone, just hold them all within your Heart and be prepared to Love them all. Be prepared to watch and to listen and to revive your Knowing.

You have been taught to prefer the familiar (which originates from a fear based ego survival mentality) and now you are going to learn that familiarity in form is not what you are looking for.

It is Light Weave connection which is your key to "at Homeness", and that connection comes from Heart Knowing.

It comes from discernment of your Truth Feeling, not from any cognitive construction or criteria.

WE are One (and We are each a unique fractal of THE ONE), no matter what shape or form or expression. And our Star Brothers and Sisters are walking amongst us right now.

Some whom you have met and are about to meet, you will be very comfortable with, and some you will have to allow to be embraced in your Love without hardly a glimpse of recognition at first.

Some will really puzzle you, and that's OK. But we are all about to learn these things very quickly and the only preparation you have is the strength of your Love and your willingness and dedication to follow the Flow of your Heart and allow and own your own expansion of consciousness, without any judgement of "For or "Against". Though it is quite natural for us to each have our own Preferences.

With meeting people it is more like a feeling "Yes Now" and "Not yet".

Start by Heart connection to all those "strangers" that live in your vicinity. Allow for the fact that you can Love, even if you cannot understand or recognise how a person can be, or see, or behave like they appear to be doing.

Shine On Galactic Beings.

ONE in God Being, through God Being, to GOD BEING.

CHAPTER 36

Set Yourself Free.

I do not let the opinions of others affect me.

I do not buy into any of the thought seeds that reflect unlovingness of others or of Self.

I seek only to empower the world and to be of service to Divine Will which is my will.

I am lovingly, playfully embracing the reality of this.

I never forgot my mother saying often "Sticks and stones can break your bones. But words can never hurt you".

And so I set myself free to me.

PS: And someone wrote to me:

"This is very lovely, Nicky, and it should be my creed. I'm too preoccupied with "someone" who has said unkind and false things about me. I really shouldn't care, but why does it still hurt? I know the truth and so does God and those who love me. Why should the opinion of one phase me at all?

And my reply:

The more you love who you are and trust yourself and your life as it is unfolding, the less you will be bothered by others. If you think no harm and no judgment of self, and you trust who you are then you will allow all others to have their own opinion of you, their own reactions and construction on their worlds.

And when you drop all the resistance you drop the need to be right, to convince them to see you differently.

I know who I am and I have no need to let others know the truth. It will be evident in my smile, my touch, my natural proclivity to express joy in the way I live.

Whatever anyone does with it is up to them. I love them anyway.

Our Human identity is changing to the childlike Truth. The fading away of the need to cling to any particular trait as defining us means that we are no longer threatened by anyone trying to tell us what we Know we are not.

The Innocence of child has become 'the Inner-sense of adult. An adult Knowing in a Child Field of expression. Unabashed, conscious without self-consciousness, free, and focussed only in the moment.

"Lest you be as a little child, you cannot enter into the Kingdom of Heaven (5D and beyond)."

CHAPTER 37

Your Purpose is to Love Being You.

Why we are here, and what we are to do (our Purpose) is all so simple.

You are here to raise your frequency in embodiment and in all you do and ARE.

It is a matter of bringing the Light of your Being, the Light of Source into your body and into everything in your life as you find it. As it 'turns up' within you and without.

Your Auric Field is like a hot air balloon.

You go higher in frequency as you drop your baggage (clear all the attachments) and blow the Light into the balloon (your entire Human body/mind field), that is ignited through conscious acknowledgement of your emotions, converted through Heart feeling (Love).

In raising your embodied frequency you automatically raise the frequency of level of thousands of others as you you're your ground in your Presence.

So your very first duty, Purpose is to Love who you are more.

To Be the Love that you ARE and invite in (consciously surrender to) the Soul Light of HUman that you can Be.

So you do not have to go anywhere, do anything but Be, embody and Live the Light of Your Love however you find it, however you wish to express it.

As Your SHINE, it will be shared wherever it is needed.

Ask of yourself in any given moment.

"How can I raise my vibration (frequency, Light quotient) in this I am experiencing? What can I do to move closer to the feeling of Joy in Being Me?"

It is all So Simple Sweet Souls.

PS: Remember, remember, and step by step learn not to be distracted from who you Truly are and have longed to be.

CHAPTER 38

World Peace: How can it be Attained?

As long as I am trying to be someone and get somewhere how could I ever know World Peace.

Peace is a state of my Being and it is nothing about attaining anything.

You are just perfect Being you, as you are, and You as you are, making your way back totally Loving everything about You.

And so how could World Peace be without me keeping my own Peace now. Peace is in the Present and the very nature of Presence, my Presence.

And if you reach for me, touch me, and stand with me you will know it, you will feel it as I will feel it Being with you.

It just IS, and cannot be contained or attained. It is Present whether felt or not. It is Presence as the very ground of your Being. You have of your on freewill an focused intention chosen to turn your LIGHT ON.

We are and have been totally addicted to drama, to "happenings", and forever seeking stimulation and distraction from the breadth of who we think we are.

How difficult it is for so many to sit wide awake, and fully Present, and be totally at Home with doing nothing?

A wonderful "practice" in fact .Or being in the Presence of others with nothing to say or to be, but there present and content.

Be Still and Know that You are God.

World Peace is quite possible and in fact inevitable.
Why? Because
You say so through who You are.

PS: And in my tears of Love for You. As I sit here writing and knowing the pain/sadness of countless sweet Souls of my Human Family ....I call to you.

Enough is enough sweet Friends.

Come to rest with the battle between your brain and your Heart.

Just Love the Precious Soul that you ARE............ PLEASE.

CHAPTER 39

Your Right to be Happy

This is a Biggy.

If your happiness is conditional on any certain outcome then you will never be happy.

It is your Divine Right to experience happiness and fulfilment. If you believe you deserve this then So It Is.

But you can only take it now in your choice of breathing, and feeling it. In any given moment you ALWAYS have a choice.

Waking up is this choice you have. To live in Love and your Lovingness or to sleep on, feeling attached to a decaying reality of yesterday.

Happiness is in the ongoing choice and unconditional expression of the Truth of your Lovingness in any now moment.

Conscious choice will inevitably blossom as state of Being. It takes quiet, gentle, nurturing, living participation, determination, persistence, patience, until your All consuming Love envelopes all that you are, and that IS, 24/7.

How committed are you to yourself and your Happiness

PS: If you find this difficult start a "Gratitude Journal" TODAY.

Put yourself on a 21 day gratitude Journey of, first thing and last thing each day to write down 5-10 things you are truly grateful for. Feel the real gratitude you have for each one of them in your life.

If you have done this before then DO IT AGAIN (no excuses).

If you think it is too simplistic then you have not properly visited the house of your Soul and tasted the Power of your Being.

Happiness is your sovereign Choice. It is your Right.

PPS: And isn't there a parallel here for the rise of HUmanity reflected in the state of the US and in fact every nation on this planet?

Is not this personal choice of one's own POWER to access Happiness also that same doorway (portal) to access Freedom?

CHAPTER 40

Some Keys for Creating.

Don't you just love synchronicities?

How everything just comes and it fits so perfectly together like it always belonged. Time and space melt and the more the love and gratitude, the more the miracles and magic. Until you only have to think or imagine and you know it is already there even if you have yet to greet it.

The Flow is always present but because we are creators of Experience, we love to imagine and to do.

In this current reality to experience the flow is to ground the thought in an action. Not to wait for circumstances to come to you or for a completed vision or clear and focussed set plans.

On little first steps in openness without desperation or overthinking.

One felt movement is all. Is all that is required to begin a monumental journey.

Grounding the insight, inspiration, or idea in action leads to materialisation whether for you or someone across the world.

It means taking it and as soon as is practical smiling, singing, speaking, dancing, touching, writing, painting, crafting it. And when doing, being open to change in direction, or totally unexpected outcome.

We feel the Flow when we are actively and totally immersed in living, connected (at One) with what is in front or by us.

Doing is the experience of unselfconscious, expanded Being in the Flow. We only feel stuck when we are waiting.

"Lightworkers" are active participants in the Flow of GOD LIGHT. All actions of the expression of Love and Creating are in the Flow.

There are no big or small expressions, there is simply you creating and in that creating is unbounded Joy.

Yes, yes sweet Friend.

And being still, and at peace and centred, is not waiting. Waiting is having an expectation of something going to happen and expecting it to come to you (which implies you are not creating it, which is an untruth).

No wonder there are a lot of "pissed off" lightworkers at the moment.

Flow will deliver, but it can't if you are not in the process of grounding (which is your initiated being in the Flow). And since Now everything has Shifted you can be in the flow all the time.

Yes, you can now open your eyes. You would have to be blind not to see.

*

CHAPTER 41

Moving from Limitation to Freedom

For Goodness Sake... LET GO.

You asked to come and take the experience of transformation.

You got the ticket when there were millions of other beings queuing up for it.

No one in Heaven or Earth can stop it ......the Transformation of Humanity, the Great Shining.

You may as well relax into it.

You asked to break free of all limitations of the fullest expression of You.

So now you have your wish.

Stop complaining about all the changes going on in yourself or "out there".

ALL limitations are being stripped away from you. It is your own journey to sovereignty so stop worrying about others.

They too are moving in the same great inexorable Stream. Each will experience this Miracle from inside to out, from their own point of view and understanding and in their own time.

Stop focusing and talking about all the "painful' experiences and start sharing your joys and appreciation in what you are experiencing.

What you repeatedly think and share you perpetuate as feedback loops that maintain your creations.

Become more aware and in conscious choice of your thoughts, and the words you use in your internal dialogue, and in your speech.

You are created from all your experience.... The good, the bad, the ugly ...and the AWESOME.

And as for Judgement.

No matter what you are experiencing you have not done anything wrong. You are on track. You just have to choose how you want it to feel, as you go through this transformation. With fear, apprehension, and worry, or with joy, gratitude, expectancy, lovingness, and Shine.

Look without and you will focus on the fading past. Feel within and you will experience the Joy of Now and the excitement of Infinite Potential to come. Freedom or worry.

How do you wish to experience the beginning of your enlightened life on New Earth?

There is no one or nothing else left that is real that you can blame. and you either know this, or are avoiding yourself, or refusing to look, or still coming out of the deep sleep.

You are in the Great Flow. Just stop struggling and float with it and with us All.

There is no one but You in there. Nothing more to clear, no more relationships to heal, no more rivers to cross or mountains to climb.

It is over, what more do you need to put yourself through to be able to say "I deserve and I am ready, let's GO.

BRING IT ON".

Enough is enough. Let Go.

CHAPTER 42

Becoming Unattached

We have not lived long enough to be able to embrace all that we have come here to experience. That is one of the many reasons we made the Shift.

The shift gives humans all the time they need to experience what they desire to manifest, and then move on.

Make friends with death. The illusion of death is dissolving with every embrace of your Love and your Knowing of your connection to All That Is.

In the waking to the eternal stream of your Soul Beingness, the veil lifts, as the Lightening of your body density, through the new HIGHER LIGHT coded "software" downloads, is enlivening and expanding your auric field and thus your awareness.

Nothing to be done as everything is being undone. Just relax a bit more.

To be here more fully is to just enjoy being you just as you ARE.

BE HERE NOW

Everything else will follow.

Welcome Home Shining One

PS: As you are now coming into alignment with Gaia in your 5th dimension Beingness, you cannot hold on to (be attached to) anything that is conditional. Your 5D Beingness does not support it and it cannot remain here. All that was conditional is dropping away from you.

Your choice is to let it go, or hold on, to old habits (the illusions of the old 3D) and continue to make yourself sick, physically, mentally, emotionally, and spiritually.

So you are experiencing this "drop away' as a losing of your old identity. And it is strange and disconcerting, but it is perfectly "normal".

Feel the freedom that this dying away brings you.

Feel the growing ease of being in the moment.

The Death of who you thought you were, and the BIRTH of all the Unknown, Infinite Potential of the AWESOME BEING YOU ARE

On any given day, everything that needs to be done you will do, and all the rest is taken care of.

CHAPTER 43
A Look into Who You are in Essence as HUman

Be kind and gentle with Yourself.

Take a good look at your own baby photo right now.

A Beautiful Precious Being, straight from God, having gone through the shock of the birth canal and being bombarded with thought forms and a myriad of emotional/mental traumas of a Collective Human dense energy field.

You had partially taken leave of the "cloisters "of your Soul Being in Spirit. Of being enwrapped in Eternal Love. So it is only natural that you would, right from the beginning, be looking for the maintenance of that GOD LOVE you had always Known.

Remember the little girl or little boy that IS your Essence of Being.

Honour them (Who You ARE).

Nurture, feel strength and Truth, of your Innocence, your Playfulness, your Curiosity, and your unbounded JOY.

Love who You are with intensity, tenderness, and fullness.

May this day, reflect the Shine of your Holy Presence on all you have been, now are, and have yet to become in your expanding Luminous Soul Self.

You are both Precious and Magnificent.

CHAPTER 44

Divine YOU is Always Present if You Allow

We have all had the experiences we needed to have to get to where we are. Your ascension, the Shift, is occurring through all us being ourselves. It is through shifting out of being "spiritual" and just being authentic.

Wearing your Heart (Knowing), "on your sleeve", through your face, and being "out there" from "in here".

Be in the acceptance of yourself.

Accept your love, accept your sadness, accept your anger, and all your feelings without stories attached to them, and be in the vibration of it as an experience and watch it change because of the very nature of who you are and the moment to moment conscious choices of how you prefer to feel.

These varieties of emotion are simply the wonderful variety of the experience of being HUman and a HUman Being.

They tell you clearly what frequency you are aligning to and signal you to watch from Soul Being, and listen deeper "within" to the navigational voice of Soul Self.

Relax, life is not happening to you, it is happening FOR YOU.

So, hand on heart, take three breaths, and tune into what is happening. There is nothing to avoid or deny it is just all about trustingly leaning into the experience, feeling the subtle tilt, and following from "inner" Soul Choice.

Whatever you are experiencing right now, you are not broken, you don't need fixing, you don't need healing, you don't need any teaching. Right now where you are, you are dwelling in the absolute perfection of your own magnificence and it is so vital that you know this.

The Divine Soul Being that you ARE, Loves you just as you are, and if you are good enough to be loved by God (SOURCE) that you are, you are good enough to be loved by YOU.

If you are really appreciating who you really are then quite naturally you will unlock the gifts, talents and abilities that are secreted within you.

End the resistance to you and just watch what happens.

Chill out. You do not have to strive to get somewhere any more. There is nowhere to go.

Right now, in this moment everything is present. The Divine YOU is always Present so you do not have to do anything but be Present to experience that Truth and take your next step into what is calling you in this next moment.

Shine On

CHAPTER 45 Shining a light on Shadow

Do not fall into the "shadow trap" of despair over events that are now being enacted on the mind/emotional "surface" of the present Human drama.

The Shadows embedded in the human psyche have to come into plain view for everyone.

The more awake you are the more you see the "Movie" as just that. And the easier and quicker it is for you to take your own Truth of "higher" ground to watch and Love, to LOVE and observe.

Shadow have worked long enough in our subconscious programming and every Shadow has to be brought to the LIGHT.

There is a Great Plan, and NONE of it (Shadow) can be missed or overlooked.

There are thousands who have worked tirelessly and Knowingly behind the scenes who understand their own part in the conquest of shadow but no One either see the whole picture nor can do it without the many.

Every protagonist of Original GOD LIGHT intention, both within each of us and imprinted on the "matrix" must be rooted out. Shadow has been very, very clever, and diabolically insidious.

We are looking at each our own shadow imprints, bringing them to LIGHT and thus every iota has to be first SEEN. And each time it is faced we make a choice. To see it, recognise and acknowledge it, and feel with all our Heart and Lovingness to say "No, this is not what I prefer. I choose FREEDOM through my own sovereignty to LOVE FEARLESSLY."

And thus You choose ......LIGHT ON.

The conscious choice of your connection to the Radiate LIGHT of GOD/SOURCE streaming down through you into the expanding Field of your own SOUL BEING as Human. And it is available to you Constantly, with every breath. Only then will you see clearly enough to step from the old world into a NEW WORLD ORDER that we are creating Together in every NOW moment.

Stay the course Beloved Friends.

There is a PLAN. It is on track. And every one of us has a unique part to play.

Shine On.

CHAPTER 46
A Declaration as a Citizen of Earth.

A Declaration as a True HUman of Planet Earth.

"I hold these Truths to be self-evident.

That All are created equal, and exist in a Field of Infinite, Unconditional LOVE and Union.

That All are endowed by their Creator with certain unalienable rights, that among these are Life, Liberty and the Pursuit of Happiness."

Please pause for a moment and say this out loud to yourself feeling the strength of its truth echoing within you.

Amend it to suit yourself and your feeling of honour, courage, and utter Love for Who you are.

You are simultaneously an Angel of LOVE and LIGHT and a Warrior of STRENGTH and COMPASSION.

Beautiful HUman.

CHAPTER 47

Embracing Our "Younger" Warriors of Light

So you are having trouble understanding your teenagers and young adults.

They are Aquarians.

They have come here not to discover your truth but to experience their own.

They have come into a reality hologram and see immediately that the old fading version makes no sense to them.

They have come with an underlining clarity of being that brings them continually into the focus of an unwillingness to participate in the sham of "normalcy" and the pain they feel when they do.

Fantasy (eg computer games) and pleasures that may heighten their senses or numb the mind are all reflections of their unwillingness to participate in the old reality.

They have come to lay bare the hypocracy and illusion.

They are passionate and single minded, mostly unafraid to step into darkness and mess with the macabre and thus at times seem to be travelling in shadow realms.

So what can we do?

We can hold the vision and knowing of who they truly are.

Starseeds, with the warrior capacity to cut through the illusion, the "bullshit", the belief systems that have imprisoned humans for ages.

Beings on a mission.

Hold that knowing and space for them. Honour their journey. You cannot make it for them. You cannot save them from themselves. They do not need it, and as you may have experienced, they do not want your help.

They are perfectly capable of walking the journey that their Being has prepared for them, even though at times it seems painful and hopeless to you.

Hold your ground, your Love and a Space for them to make their own way. How and when they take the Power of their Truth is up to them.

LOVE them vehemently, Passionately but set them Free to Be.

Aquarians desire wholeheartedly to experience in the NOW. And if we are to do anything for them it would be to provide them with more open opportunities to experience themselves in New Ways.

They will find themselves in that experiencing.

Your own joy in your experience is the most powerful way you can touch them. Let them see who YOU really are and then they will have a more accurate measure to gauge their own flight back into themselves when they are ready.

Through your great Love and honour for them. They will feel SEEN. Then it will be easy and relatively quick for them when they make their move into their LIGHT.

Simply Shine

PS: Many in the older generation will also recognize much of this description as themselves. All the more reason to be able to hold the space for our beautiful younger ones.

And perhaps they are present in your life, not so much to learn from you, but to present you with gifts of the deepening of your own Heart and your Knowing of what your Compassion can allow. The Truth of really "setting them free".

CHAPTER 48

Your World Needs You

Our Thrival depends on diversity.

That means you and I are to honour our uniqueness and our difference. Each a unique gift of the One. A fractal of an ever expanding Creation .

This is the change we have been watching and listening for. It is here. It is you and it is me.

We are here Remembering. And it is in the Joyful Sharing and the Shining that our planet becomes Fun and a Sun.

So no one has "THE" answers. The solution to anything is held in the unfolding, blending hearts of all humanity. It is in the doing from Being.

All resolutions are in the evolving Whole. They have never been in mental/logical construction and planning.

Solutions are in an "organic", fluid movement not in static structure. They are in unconditional expansion not in conditional separation.

And the brilliant little lights of awakening HUmans are popping up everywhere.

Do you see them in your own neighbourhood?

Do you feel the excitement as the Shining Ones arise?

It is Global for we have spoken and So It Is.

Shine On

PS: The time is Now when humanity, all around you, needs you. Needs to feel the calm, the steadfastness, the Love and Compassion, the Faith and the Hope of someone whose gaze and Heart is clearly fixed on their Soul Beingness and a New Earth Dream.

To be Present with, to sooth the SHOCK, the fear, the hurt, the anger and the utter undermining of much that they believed as True.

To be a 'working part" of the Great Reveal.

To sooth with the calm of Loving Kindness rather than deluge them with new information and beliefs systems.

ARE YOU READY?

Your people need you.

CHAPTER 49
A New Way of Being

You are the Story Teller.

What New Story are you writing for yourself to live the next Chapter of your Dream?

Visions, dreams, imaginings at any time are visions for that time.

The question is how deeply, truly, constantly do you Believe or Know them?

The energies and the potentials for the future are written only in your beliefs (fear or joy based) or the Knowing of your Heart (wisdom and love based).

However, there are many potential futures, and like pages of a book, events can be turned to reveal an entirely new chapter. They are not carved in stone, only through the clarity, and constancy of your own Heartsong.

Things can change in the twinkling of an eye when we change our beliefs. We have that much power.

Materialisation of what we believe in may take some time to appear in density but the strength, clarity and constancy of your visions is the assurance that So Be It. When the alignment between you and your Dream is right Miracles happen.

So what future do you want? It can only be crafted and built in the Present. Align with it now, align with it as an open portal, more as a question than an answer. "What is the possibility of ……. Show me Universe. Thankyou, thankyou." Asking yourself often "What if…..?"

And believe it is so with all your heart, and surrender and allow, and receive all the synchronicities and experiences that will lead you to it. Feel it deep within your Heart and milk it well for the immediate feelings of enjoyment your Dream brings you.

Look and listen for the signs, keep your vision. See the reality you are creating through the "appearances and disappearances" of the old. When your belief becomes a knowing that is strong enough and your heart is constant, the reality you are experiencing "within" becomes the "without".

There is this Shift. And behold the Miracle.

You are a Creator Being Beloved Storyteller.

CHAPTER 50
Finding Your True Love

DID YOU KNOW?

That ever since you were a child you were frightened into believing that you are not good enough and somehow you had done something wrong.

That you had to find a way of pleasing others to fit in and to be loved

That no matter what you have done, searching for something outside yourself, could never work nor satisfy your yearning to be Truly seen and to be Loved.

That your Soul Presence (Who You ARE) has never been fully present in your body.

That the fear that is in your body has kept you from being fully Present and becoming the Happy, Playful, Free Soul and HUman THAT YOU TRULY ARE.

That you are taking back this Divine Union .....NOW..

This Divine Marriage masculine/feminine, of body and Soul, of Light and Form, of particle and wave, of Child of Innocence and Wisdom, melding as ONE.

You are immersed in this entire INVOLUTIONARY continual 'process'. An absolutely Natural one.

And it inevitability is out of your hands because you are here on an Ascended Planet. You have already in Truth made your Choice.

Every frequency that is not aligned to 5D+ has gone except those held in the Auric Fields (and subconsciousness) of the Human consciousness. So it is "Shape Up or Ship Out" time.

There is No One to Blame anymore once you realise that you are Soul Being coming into Beautiful HUman and you had a preordained plan to SHINE as a unique Point of LIGHT in the Mind of GOD on this Precious little Blue Planet

You as Human have to take hold of your WILL to focus your entire consciousness, and surrendering the reins to whatever comes up (the "outer) in your life.

And you process your part in the simplest of ways.

Whatever comes up that is not in alignment with Joy, you Observe, you see it for what it is. Your body will tell you. No analysis simply observation.

Then watch as it dissolves. And this can be very quick.

It will be in your Stillpoint, in Divine Neutrality, that dissolution, resolution, transformation will occur miraculously.

And as it does We say "Thankyou, thankyou, now I Know" and Smile within ourselves.

You are not going Home.

You are COMING HOME to YOU in emBODYment.

Your body KNOWS. It is leading you constantly.

Do the work.

There can no longer be any half measure without immediately feeling the consequences. Conscious, Open, all Embracing FAITH.

And the LOVE That You Are applied to the journey of your own experience

CHAPTER 51

Creating a New World Together

The appearances of our "outer" 3D Human Collective reality is splitting apart into countless fragments.

What you used to think as real, and gave you the reality of some thought of "reliability", can no longer be. There is no place for it to be.

The "new" energy of the 5th Root Race of Humankind has now a firm "foothold" (Heart embrace really), as the Flow of the Shift to a Golden Age begins to unfold in the "outer world", as we let go of what appeared to be, and take back, in ever unfolding Knowings, our Longings, our Dreams, our deep Preferences for Living the Days of our Hero Destiny.

There is so much pain, hurt and grief, to be released for so many.

STAND UP.

Be counted. Not for your hate of a contrived system conceived in the Shadows and daily baiting you into self-doubt and fear from within, but for your Love and Trust in God, Yourself, and for the main body of your HUman Family.

It is crucial in these next months and years that you find, in any way you can, how to be and remain INSPIRED.

We are not waking up to have to run the "gauntlet" of pain and opposition anymore. We are awakening to our own sovereign Freewill choice to see and be, to live and Love, in community of creative, joyful expression always in touch with our inner Calm and Gratitude.

This where we help each other. We remind and sit beside our Soul Families. To be fully Present and to hold the Inner Smile of always Knowing how Loved we are, how Lovable, and how Loving.

You are HUman and You are Love Incarnate.

And in the Innocence of your Knowing you can Imagine your new world into being.

Hold, play, and expand in your visions together, unperturbed by the "external appearances" arising from the Shadows. Playing out as knots of ignorance, manipulation, and confusion totally unravelling and fading away. .

Love always finds a way even when there appears to be no way.

Love Fearlessly.

The Great Plan is Mighty, beyond words, and there are millions around the globe, in every walk of life, whose paths have led them to be in the right place for the right time.

We do this Together.

Stay the course.

Go into your Stillness. And hold the Eternal LIGHT within you, with increasing Confidence, and Contentment.

CHAPTER 52

How to Master these Times.

There is a great bifurcation going on in the Human consciousness.

We are all having to make the choice LIGHT ON or LIGHT OFF.

All are being challenged, and being tested. Each at their own level of understanding, whether they appear "awake or still sleeping".

Can you stay the course and are you firmly committed to the LOVE that You are through and through.

Are you choosing to step into a New World of your dreams, imagination and longing, without knowing what will come next, but bring forward into your daily sight your Hopes and Longing, through an unshakeable Faith in God (an Eternal Benevolent Source) and the Love that YOU ARE.

Or will you try and control life on a kind of autopilot, where the possibilities of a good and happy life is dependent on the actions of a Collective ,"out there" reality.

This is how I Choose

It is thus, that when I slow myself right down, clarity emerges. LIGHT switches ON.

As we slow down, into Quiet Mind, with repetition, Awareness becomes "laser" focused.

Then everything becomes available in plain sight.

So simple really.

On the way

At Home inside.

Joy in your step.
And Heart open wide.

CHAPTER 53

Finding the Courage to be Vulnerable.

To own, define and experience our own Auric (Electro-magnetic) Field is so central to what happens in these times.

As human we have been so used to giving away our power or protecting it.

Your Radiance is exactly that, ...YOUR Radiance. No one can take it away from you and it is limitless and boundless.

So it is time to discover all the ways you subtly give away your power, and take it back. At the same time drop your protection. You are totally worthy and all power unto yourself.

Own your own Soul Presence. That within you which Watches the 'movie" out there all the time. That which is your own Radiance. Without any excuse or any game/story whatsoever. Being totally unafraid to love yourself and every other Being without any need to hold back who you are and what your preferences are.

It is surprising how much energy you have expended in trying to hold back the expression of your JOY.

Remember being vulnerable is not being weak. It goes with aliveness and wholeheartedness. It is being willing to be totally exposed with the Knowing of your eternal connectedness to All That Is, and a fearless commitment to You being You.

It goes with Loving Yourself.

Shine On

PS: "SAFE" is a 3D mindset which says you need protection.

But you are a Soul Being of Infinite Light. There is no "UNSAFE" in 5D (Unconditional Universal God LOVINGNESS).

Are you prepared to be here?

If "yes" then what is vulnerability? The capacity to Jump in to the Unknown and discover more of who you are. More of your magnificent power to Create what you truly long for and desire.

CHAPTER 54

Love to Places of Conflict in Our World.

I intend that freedom, unity, friendship, community and abundance descend on ALL countries and dissolve the fear, grief, anger and confusion.

That the despots give up their hopeless cause of greed, manipulation, hate, and hurt, and their hearts melt as they are contained in the LOVE we have for ALL.

From here, I will to Love conflict to "death".

Beloved friends send a triple solar flare (heart, mind. and gut (solar plexis)) from your Radiance to the heart Radiance of any place of conflict that comes to mind, and the precious HUman Hearts that are there.

Shine, Shine, Shine, the power of your Love, Beloved Friends. The illusion is dissolving.

We, the people, are doing it.

Just know this to be so within your own Life as you find it. and be patient and steadfast.

Do not believe the misguided warmongerers caught in the realms of Shadow, who would like to stir up your fear and anger, confusion and self-doubt.

Thankyou, thankyou, Brothers and Sisters, of all countries, beliefs, and persuasions, for holding your ground at last, for your birthright of Freedom, Unity, and LOVE.

The Middle Eastern, Asian and African, and South American lands are the cradles of HUman civilization, they held our magical dreams and solid hopes, and now we hold those same, and share back the gifts that those peoples have given us.

We so Love you.

No thought of Love or a breath of Light is ever wasted.

We are all so powerful, and together we are shifting the mountains of fear. Dissolving them with our Love just as a river dissolves the mountain rock.

Folks of the world be patient and use your Heart Power, we are watching a miracle happen. Or should I say creating that miracle?

PS: Know that your heart felt thoughts of Love connect you to the WWW of LOVE that is palpable now. And as we love, we serve, we create, we transform, using each our gifts. It is the Now reality of 5th dimensional Being (Unconditional Universal, Eternal LOVE) and Living.

AND SO IT IS.

CHAPTER 55

We "Fell" Because We Ignored our Heart Knowing.

And the so called "fall" of Humanity happened very simply through "vanity.

A Group of Humans listening to their Shadow voices, thought they could do it all without God, without Divinity, without their very own Essence.

And we were each convinced (against our higher knowing) and have taken the whole idea/reality that we could do it through the "Mind", and through controlling life, and we forgot the Heart, we forgot that creating is an endless unfolding of our dreams. That it is miraculous, and magical and is initiated in the (child) Innocence that was our birthright.

The Atlantean peoples had it all and learned to create anything in form. They knew health, wealth and happiness but they eventually thought that they could do it without their Godhead. That in their spiritual arrogance they put all their trust in the tools (especially crystals). The grand separation.

And it destroyed them all.

Now we are undoing it, retracing the fall in reverse, through Love. In moving back to the Heart of ONE first, we are discovering that health, wealth and happiness, and creative genius must follow. It Just IS.

Don't try to grab anything. If you are creating it will arrive in the Divine timing and the manifestation that you are a part of. If you need to cultivate one thing for this all to happen then let it be Loving, joyful patience in total FAITH that the Divine GOD SOURCE within You is doing all the 'heavy lifting'.

PS: All that is miscreation is being revealed. All Shadows are coming out front (being reveal). It has to when the Light of your Truth is Shining. All that is vain and self-serving must be revealed.

And maybe your reluctance of declaring fully your own Magnificence is an ancient fear of your own vanity. Vanity is your ultimate shadow which you now know and can Love the Knowing of.

So until you claim who you truly are before all Creation, the Light and the truth and your fullness of Presence waits within you. If you know the difference between vanity and the Truth of You as the Holy of Holy, then step boldly Beloveds. Allow your High Soul Self to flood your consciousness and enter your body, to take sovereignty and be fully immersed.

CHAPTER 56
The Joy in following Your Heart.

In the current chaos there is infinite possibility, and you have the opportunity, as never before to make a permanent shift from fear to excitement.

I love the way that following Heart and my inner knowing and promptings, without any specific reason, or need for a reason, always leads to more Me, more You, and MORE Awesome.

And if I cannot give mind to where I am going, how can I explain or justify it to you. And why should I feel I have to?

Around the corner out of sight in this very next moment is "something", a surprise, a delight, awaiting your embrace.

There is absolutely no way that YOU can be not OK.

CHAPTER 57

The Mastery of Non-Judgement

I know who I AM and you will find me as you wish. If you judge me you limit yourself to who I can be for you.

It has no bearing on who I will be to myself.

Do you get this?

The last thing to go for the open Heart of HUman is judgement of the worth of others.

When fully connected to your Source (the Eternal LIGHT and LOVE of GOD) you will Know your worthiness, your beautiful Innocence.

Be the observer of Self today. And with total honesty and without censure simply be aware every time you make a judgement of the worth others.

And tomorrow do the same until it goes down to zero.

This is real self-Mastery.

CHAPTER 58

The Wisdom of the Human Collective.

There is a "place, space" in the here and now, where and when the HUman hologram, the collective consciousness "resides". It is like the Soul of the Collective HUman Dream. And it is unfolding its infinite narrative as we each express the potentials of who WE are.

People ask me where my daily writing come from.

I do not consider myself a "channel". I simply have called that part of me that is at One, at Home with HUmaness, the "WE". It is the place I speak from within me. I AM in Awe to serve in this manner.

And so each day a flavour of this connection of Our common dream is translated by me through the WE, as it were, and I share with you now. That is why often the words appear fortuitous, synchronous, appropriate, and familiar. For it expands from Our Dream and I invite you to bring it more consciously into your awareness.

WE are all so brilliantly "entangled".

Our Collective Consciousness (the Song of the HUman Dream) is about our potential to Love more and in the creative expression and expansion of that love, to weave New Patterns of Dreams that will allow ever more expansive experience of our shared joy.

Shine On

WE So Love You

PS: So as the battle of dark/light plays out, just as a narrative of the old human collective dream plays out in "little mind". But there is great possibility for the New Earth Dream of the Collective to be brought forward from within the Genius of our combined Hearts.

It is and must be through the individual and Freewill choice of each and every one of us.

Regardless of what "side' you take, the "battle" will continue while you "fight from the trenches" hidden in the shadows of your old life in the human collective.

I am maintain that you have to move to" higher ground" (go to the peace and Love of God, that you are) to see with clarity and discernment the Whole picture.

In every moment you make this CHOICE to See with the Eyes of Love, all your resistance fades away. You are no longer a victim to the Shadow which would have you believe that you have been "wronged", by anything that is not your own ego mind.

How foolish it is keep complaining that "doors have been closed" and cannot be opened until someone else changes their mind. Who has dominion over your mind.

When you choose to go and] look from "higher ground" you will always see an Open Door.

LOVE (GOD) will always show it to you even though it may appear at first sight there is none.

You cannot be betrayed by anyone but Yourself.

CHAPTER 59

Time to Step Up

It is ironic how so many Lightworkers have been dragged into the fear mongering after having been told and actively welcoming the thought of a Great Awakening.

Think how magnificent it is that All Humanity is stirring, from a slumber of ages, and are being presented with the opportunity to truly know themselves and make self-empowering freewill life choices.

It is beginning to happen as foretold by sages and seers through the Ages.

So in order for each to gain their Freedom, as foretold long ago, there is now great tumult and tribulation, fear and confusion amongst the people. A clinging desperately to the old energy and a volatile reaction to those who are not.

And this is where You and I are supposed to come in.

It is perhaps the greatest reason why you are Here in these momentous times.

To Go OUT THERE into the market place and walk your walk and share your calm and happy Presence.

The time has come to STEP OUT.

And not shout your Truth, but Shine in your own way having made your Freedoms Choice.

No touch too small where Love is present.

Your people need you

It is no longer enough to be just a 'Lightworker'. It is now time to be the WAYSHOWER. Of your first Choice.... Your Light within (God) and then service to others....... OR.......

Possession of "outer appearances of wealth and power (Mammon) and service to self.

The people need the Touch of your Love and your Calm and seeing you Fearless and without judgement.

Not long lectures as to Your Truth to prove your 'rightness".

Just You demonstrating in your Presence what Your Choice brings you.

Just be YOU Being YOU every day.

Willingly, Lovingly and Fearlessly.

CHAPTER 60

Standing Firmly in Embodiment, I AM

Compassion resides in your knowing of the Love that you are.

It is your connection to all. So how could anyone be left out of your embrace?

It is an ever expanding embrace, and energy match, not an energy exchange. Nothing can be lost because everything is included.

Stepping back into yourself is not stepping away from anyone. It is actually the reverse.

Reaching down into the depth of You, you find the WE that you are.

Sure you feel a distancing but this is merely the breaking of attachments and hooks, disengaging from old mind sets and the dissolving emotional filters and the freeing of yourself, and of others to be themselves.

As you let go, surrender, everything comes easier.

This is you stepping into your own energetic field. Discovering the fathomless multidimensional experience of SOUL SELF.

This is You in the FLOW.

Your caring is not in the giving of your energy, it is in the expression of your SELF. Your heartfelt Knowing guiding the Love that you are.

You will feel so different now, in the 'drawing away' from so many people and in the unselfconscious sharing of who you are (your Truth).

Service to Self now contains within it service to All.

It will almost "hurt" in the freedom of it, but it will make so much sense once you have let go of any need to interpret it. We could say it is Being at Home in SELF.

You will be "lifted up", just like floating in a lucid dream like state, while still residing in the body, and feet firmly on the ground, as you come Home to your immediate knowing.

You "lighten up" in all senses of the phrase. Less is more.

No more "trying". Life with the ease that FAITH brings.

You cannot understand with your mind so surrender to the inner knowing, the knowing in the feeling of "rightness". You are learning to "see" with the new eyes of the Open Heart.

You are learning to be fully plugged into Essence of you, and in that, connected to everyone.

The inner Glow and the outer Shine.

CHAPTER 61

Clearing the 'Past'.

So much is being said about "clearing" yourself of the dross, the density, and the past stories and feelings that arise within you.

So much is being presented as "activations" to make you "more" than what you think you are.......so many, methods, modalities and "experts" who can bring keys to your "enlightenment, evolution and frequency upgrade", etc, etc.

Where do you begin, how do you choose, and where does it end?

I Love SIMPLE.

So let me give you another point of view that may or may not be helpful to you.

Your past in this now moment (4D) is composed of memories. Thoughts that arise of experiences you have had. Thoughts that you presently contain in your conscious and unconscious data banks bodily, emotionally and mentally.

Thoughts are electric and each has a surrounding magnetic charge we call "emotions" (Energy in MOTION). So when a thought arises it brings for you the visceral experience that you have attached to it when you first experienced the event that created it, most often other people's instructions on how you should see something to "fit in", or how you project what others "might" be thinking, or the emotions others had at the time that you 'picked up' the thought.

So now as you Wake Up (begin to become fully Conscious 24/7), the memories and the thoughts that support these memories come into your conscious experience along with the emotions attached to them. They are "triggered" by an event when they are ready to be released.

And here is the BIG BUT.

They are only memories, well worn neural paths, that are electromagnetic. They stand for your interpretation of experiences and were given their charge by You when you were very young and Innocent.

So "clearing" is simply experiencing the charge as the emotion, the visceral feeling, rises in you, and breathing it into your Heart, the Heart of One, the Heart of Your Lovingness, where there is an embrace, an instantaneous total acceptance. The you can "wave it goodbye" because in feeling it consciously, it comes out of the Shadows into the Light of your Knowing. As you smile for that Knowing, or appreciate, or simply observe the memory, and allow and let go, the experience of the feeling (and its emotional charge) are now released to become part of your active Chi (Lifeforce). It is transmuted into the field of your Lovingness.

DONE AND DUSTED.

No fanfare, no special skill, no deep analysis, just being Present, a deep breath, and a Loving observation of allowing and understanding.

In doing this you have Observed it from the point of Soul Being. In a Love without judgement of yourself or the other players in this bygone event. We might call this "forgiveness ". Forgiveness for you taking on something which was not really anything to do with the Truth of who you are,

And as for activation, sure there are helpful tips and loving hearts that are out there to offer their experience of the guidance they receive.

However, as I see it, they can only hold the 'Truth Light of their own experience and in that Presence (and Forgiveness) they can "point to" a way that they have found their "open door" to their own Lovingness.

Your ascension, your "waking up", your conscious perfect alignment of self to the Divine You, and the Divine You to HUman self, is already preordained and well underway because you have chosen (Willed) it.

There is nothing missing and you will miss nothing.

Your journey "back" into SELF is "preprogrammed", as it were, from the magnificence connection of Soul Being to God and Soul Being to Beautiful HUman that you are in your unique Hero's journey.

You, in league with Source have already set it up.

We could call it "FLOW". And thus perhaps the only "activation" required is you being totally committed to Loving every bit of YOU. A conscious, active and full participation in this Now, in awareness of what is going on "inside" you, and in the expansion of your own Lovingness.

Everything, YES, everything will follow quite naturally, quite perfectly, quite miraculously.

It is the 'failsafe' Law of your own Ascension.

So for Heaven Sake!........... RELAX.

And stop searching for your flaws, shadows, etc. If you are open and honest with yourself, and have chosen to be Heart Centered, your trajectory and the signs will appear daily and perfectly in their own good (God) time.

You are Coming Home Beautiful HUman.

Shine On

CHAPTER 62

Be Still "I Am God".

Having trouble meditating?
 Take around 20 minutes EVERY DAY.
 Make time and do not listen to your own excuses.
 Sit and do nothing else. Don't daydream. Don't go off on a tangent, just time with yourself and do Nothing.
 As thought arise just watch them. When you thoughts arise simply become aware that you are "thinking" and let go of whatever thoughts you are having. Keep coming back to the stillness that is always behind thought.
 After a while you really will begin to enjoy it and something very subtle will begin to happen in your life and in you.
 It takes time and great patience with yourself.
 Do nothing but be Present and watch the magic.
 Or you can do the same thing going for a walk or doing a repetitive chore.
 Waking up is being consciously aware and Present. Nothing else.
 The depth of experience is commensurate with the depth of stillness and increased ability to make choice of no thought in any moment.
 Stilling the mental mind eventually has to be mastered. When you can sit quietly and simply watch and Be, then PRESENCE appears.
 Your most Holy Presence, the Presence of All That Is.
 It is not a one time thing. It is to become the very Essence of you Being YOU

PS: And I know so many of you have tried and feel you have failed but not so, sweet readers. There is a readiness for everything. Take the time often to sit with yourself and be still and just watch what is there.

Say to yourself, "Out there is a movie, and who is seeing it is Soul Being I AM". Then watch.

And when thoughts are rampant just watch and as soon as you notice that you are immerse in thought distraction, whatever it may be, you are back again with yourself.

If it is really difficult, then simply take a two syllable sound, that has no particular meaning (eg "om shanti", or "ah um", or "so hum", etc, etc) and repeat it over and over in your mind (not out loud). Keep doing it. Each time a taught or string of thoughts comes and you are aware of them go back to repeating the sound until there is only this sound and nothing else.

When there is thought, back to this sound (mantra). I guarantee you will always feel a lovely Peace filled, content, "warm fuzzy' shift after each of your sessions.

As you persist you will go deeper, and it will begin to flow into your day more and more and I cannot tell you the beauty you will rediscover.

Why would I want to spoil the surprises in store for you.
BE STILL
I AM THAT I AM
And
THOU ART THAT

PPS: No meditative guided talk, no music, simply you with YOU.

CHAPTER 63

The Gift of You

These things you know.

There is much cleansing that has been done. More and more people are Awakening and drawing their lines in the sands of what is acceptable and unacceptable to them. It becomes clearer that there are personal boundaries and that their Spiritual awareness is experiencing too much input from the external World around them and thus they are learning to withdraw, take back and define their own Life.

Many will look to your light for guidance for they will sense the difference between Truth and Presence, and the old ego patterns and mindsets.

Your personal well-being matters, and I see more and more people are doing all that they can, to ensure that they have a peaceful sanctuary where they can go to recharge rejuvenate, and align with themselves.

As conduits of the higher frequency energies (Spirit), much energy replacement needs to take place within our physical bodies.

Always listen to the signals your body is giving you and follow its direction.

Look deep within you.

Practice the attitude of gratitude, for it will help you so much during these intensely changing times, because the thoughts put out into the Universe is what the Universe will give back to you in your Now.

Minding (paying attention to) the thoughts you consciously choose to have is a major key to creating the World you desire to live in. Becoming more and more aware of your 'within' to become the 'without'.

What you constantly dwell on in your thoughts will bring the manifestation of that into your daily life very quickly in one form or another in order to meet the requirements of your creative alignment. This is especially true in the relationship with your inner feelings and events that bring you the opportunity for more of that feeling.

Your past is now irrelevant to who you are Now. That is a matter of choice because you recreate yourself in every moment. And gratitude will evolve into a constant feeling of return to Joy and appreciation for All That Is.

It will become the most beautiful attitude within you of the preciousness, the sacredness, and the connectedness to all Life and the Knowing that you are an essential and magnificent part of it All. And more properly It is an essential and magnificent part of YOU.

Follow the promptings of your heart, because it is your "higher" Heart center that is the most powerful and active of all the 'chakras' in your four 'lower' body frequencies at this time of change.

The force of Love you are gathers momentum to create miracles of transformation within your body at all levels of your Being.

The ups and downs you have been experiencing in energy levels and within your emotions is an indication that your heart centre is becoming wide open and this increases the feeling of vulnerability within you, for in the past you have learned to protect your heart in order to shield it from the pain of rejection, betrayal, sadness, deception and separation.

This is no longer necessary and in fact creates much "dis ease".

Your task is to move beyond the fear, the mind rationalizations, and the reaction games, and let your true inner Soul Self become manifest through becoming your own Guiding Light (supported by your vast Company of Heaven) as you go about your daily life, and hold great FAITH that as you become more conscious of it you are always surrounded and infused with Love, protection and guidance in all facets of your lives.

Create this knowing and ground it in your life by speaking it out loud to yourself (In the beginning was the Word.).

Remember we are all in this together and when you go down there are always others of us right beside you who are up, and holding the space for you to gently rise again.

WE are One.

Shine On

CHAPTER 64

On Inspiring ("Helping") Others.

First and foremost, if you are in your Shining, in your Presence, then you have already brought the greatest gift you could to those you are in the company of.

In your countenance, your Smile, through your eyes, from your heart, comes the magic of Flow which even a fractional part of others knows full well.

And so in essence there is nothing to do, nothing that has or needs to be said for The Gift to be given. It can pass "unseen and unheard", yet is felt, heart to heart.

When I first started my counselling and therapy work, 50 years ago, I resolved to trust my training to the Universe and trust the "patient/client/searcher/seeker" to bring to me what they needed for me to help them with, and to trust myself that what I did would lead to the most benevolent outcome for all concerned.

I cannot remember it ever not working. When someone comes, I remember that they are not broken (they are Divine and perfect), they do not need "fixing". It was essentially a transaction from "Soul Self to Soul Self. There was no system or theory or conceptualised work that was indispensable.

My FAITH in life trained me and those who came and still come to me are my teachers.

How beautiful is that? How amazing are they?

No wonder I am in awe of HUman Nature and cannot buy into human weakness but see mostly the strength of the HUman Spirit. I see the whole "veil " is simply something we have bought into, the unkind lie that we are not to be trusted. Which is saying we are not Divine and Creators of all that we experience. A belief that HUman is small and insignificant.

There were times when I scared myself at the things I said to people (like telling someone to "grow up, take their life in hand, rather than play poor me, and to go away").

Of course I doubted often, and I still look to be aware of my ego mind that would hide myself behind fear and and self-preservation, it is part of being HUman.

Truly being with others is mostly doing and being together in that moment and not preconceiving what you are going to do or say to them, how you want the experience to go, or preempting the reaction or the outcome for you or the other. To be open to the unknown potential of the encounter.

You mind your own business and let them mind their own. So when they have gone from your presence there is no deep post-mortem. Just trust, Knowing love, and an expanded feeling of Joy, for the honour of knowing them.

What I am saying is if you Love and are open and trust yourself, and trust that the other person will show you what they are deeply asking to be reflected back to them, then there is absolutely no reason to be afraid of what you might say to anyone. You will always do the right thing by them even if they get peeved, slam the door in your face, break down and cry their heart out, or get up and hug you and fall in love with you.

The power of love works miracles even if a person goes away and you never see them again.

I have seen time and again the result of these miracles of transformation through self-empowerment, even as feedback to me 20-30 years later.

Love is never ever wasted. It is the truth and the proof of free energy.

You are Love Incarnate and so you can do anything. If you really know the power in your own freedom then that is what you can gift others by your mere Presence. The knowing and the loving are the expanding energy that calls to like frequency in the field of another.

There is no longer any need to be afraid of ego if you befriend it. You have learned well how to be aware. The ego is a most beautiful safeguard and keeps us awake to our own process at this time of being in HUmaness.

PS: And so often when someone comes I hear the voice speaking loud and clear ..."All they need is to really, really feel SEEN , and be HELD" in the arms of Love".

And when you do this by really being fully Present in the Love that you are, with them, and unafraid to let your Lovingness hold them just for a moment, they will experience what they have always longed for. And it will at last be "REAL" and open again for them.

CHAPTER 65

Straight Talk, to Precious Soul that You Are.

It is not just what we do, but how we do it that counts.
Do you feel your Lovingness?
Can you see your world through the Eyes of Your Love?
Do you Believe totally in the Power of Love to transform?
Our believing/knowing, and our doing is our BEING.
There is an I, a Me, and there is WE.
And through the ME of WE the New World is created.
Anything that has one iota of separateness in it is not of WE.
Service to others is embedded in service to Soul (Self) through HeartMind.

PS: I am seeing so many still struggling with family. Struggling with the need to be understood (and thus loved in the way you want it) with those who you know full well are bound into their own views of what the world "is" and who you are not.

Your clinging to these old stories, and persisting in taking what they say so very personally, is a continuation of reflecting back to yourself the unkind lie that you are not YOU.

They are the gift to you at this time.

You asked to awaken and WE say time and again, awakening is the realization that you are Love, you could not be anything else, nor have you been anything else but playing a game of hide and seek with yourself.

Who cares what others say or think about me. I certainly DON'T. Unless it is really about me, which is never if I am not reacting, and is about some self-judgment I am holding if I am reacting.

What YOU think about YOU, and how deeply fully and magnificently you can Love who you have been, who you are becoming, and WHO YOU ARE, is a total and profound commitment.

Your family will "GET IT" when they are ready to "get it". Bless their hearts.

Stop clinging to your own unkind lie, and a need for some unrequited love that is owed you, and taking their own hurting personally because it is projected at you.

If you Know who you are there is no way you could be shifted from that Knowing. So if there is still wavering, Beloved HUman, then there is simply more Honouring and Loving being Self to be done.

CHAPTER 66

At Home with the Ups and Downs of Life

I am not in alignment all day every day.

I AM a Soul Being "DESCENDING" (projecting consciousness into HUman embodiment and as such I have heaps of "good" moments and far less not so "good" moments.

But I know when I am out of alignment and I know how to get back.

Mostly I am quick and sometimes I am slower.

And this Nicky fellow is totally committed to aligned to non-separation (24/7).

There is always a coming back to stillness and "watching" in expanded Being of IAM and through the WE of ME.

Sometimes I will understand at a totally conscious "level" the "cause" that is always in my own doing and Being.

And often in the watching and allowing I create portals in which "shift" happens.

But I know the incredible feeling of Flow.

The beauty and fullness of ME and the WE of me.

And so I ride the waves, and sometimes I dive right into them, and it is so awesome to be HUman.

CHAPTER 67

Lighten Up

We are becoming fully conscious.

Think what that means.

Conscious, aware, focused and clear in every moment of Now.

Would you not agree that you have a lot of living and experiencing to do yet to get even close.

It unfolds step by step for you.

But the joy and Awesomeness in the journey means there need not be impatience anymore.

It is probably more now about giving yourself permission to have fun and share your laughter and tears without having to "fix" anything or anyone else.

And in the letting go everything begins to fit together in a Magnificent, Magic and Miraculous way.

Why not make it a regular habit to treat it all more playfully and less seriously.

CHAPTER 68
A Word on "Ascension".

Your Awakening, your Remembering does not happen as a blinding flash, or waiting on the threshold looking through a peephole hoping for someone to invite you in, nor can you discover your Mastery by expecting someone else to recognise you first.

How can they when you have not even acknowledged yourself? Your own Shining Divinity.

It is seeping through and into all that you are and all that you experience as Beautiful HUman.

Gently, softly, stealthily, continually.

As a warming Glow of Being. Sometimes joyous and exuberant, often quietly smiling and contemplative.

Always receptive, always embracing. Profoundly filling and gradually moving all your feeling, seeing and knowing.

And it comes easily, no more pushing because it is here within and around you simply for the receiving and the taking.

The more you sense it, the more that you beckon, the more you invite, the more you own it, the more you realise that that Glow, that radiance, that Light, IS YOU.

The flow is within you, all around you, it IS YOU.

You are Heart, the Heart of all things, All That IS.

There is nowhere to go, nowhere special to be.

You ARE, and ALL comes and goes as a most beautiful FLOW.

The Flow of YOU.......... The melding of WE.

The so called "clearing" just happens, no need to dig and delve, and explain, and direct. Just observing, watching, allowing. An ever increasing Loving wakefulness.

Wakefulness is becoming conscious of your own Soul Being.

CHAPTER 69

All the Old Stuff is Leaving if You will Allow.

So you still seem to be dealing with old issues that you thought you had cleared.

No you have not failed, you are still well and truly on track. As a fully conscious being you are becoming totally familiar with all the nuances of mind and emotion and you are to become a Master of your Mind. You have done your time being "lost" in 3D.

Stop SEEKING.

You have arrive on the Ascension "platform". Everything is arising, step by step by Divine Design, the Law of Your Own Unfolding. You simply need to TURN UP, BE PRESENT and open hearted.

And all the Old Stuff is coming up. Why? BECAUSE IT IS LEAVING.

This includes Everything that you see "out there" in the human "movie". Which is locked into a system that has no energy that supports it any longer.

You are transforming DENSITY through your body. Watch and LET GO.

If you "lock" yourself into your own Fearless, Loving, Freewill Beingness you do so for the whole HUman Collective. You lock yourself into the Benevolent Conditions underlying All Change you see going on "out there". You automatically align yourself to the New World Earth Dream such that whatever is emerging from the Shadows of human experience is turned "upside down" (reverse) even if you cannot see how. Look beneath the shadow elements, Divine Light of our intentions is working Its "magic" and miracles". Be steadfast in your Faith and Trust of God Force.

You have the power to create from any thought. So you are creating your world through the thoughts and feelings you own as that which you have the longing and desire to create.

If someone hurts you, you are rerunning the thoughts that created the hurt feeling in the first place. Choose heart then 'Watch" the thoughts and emotions, they are just thoughts and energy and you can change them anytime you choose.

We once took all the Stuff "out there" personally but we just cannot do this anymore, and the great gift is that if you allow even the smallest reaction it hurts so much because its lack of resonance with your Truth reverberates through every cell in your body.

Let it leave with hardly any attention. Do it in the moments that they arise in. Stop looking for them. Since there is only now and that is the only place you can be, you can create, in that moment.

Hurt is feeling unloved. Turn it around, always turn it around. Instead of "they hurt me" feel where the feeling is and then say "I hurt me". "I hurt me when I said............." you told yourself an unkind lie about you and then you believed it.

Remember, everyone does things or says words that are hurtful because they are hurting.

And these lies have mostly occurred through others thoughts that came when you were a child and were given little power to develop your own beliefs. It was thought that directed it and since you did not want to take your own power (for whatever reason) you projected your own feelings onto the world and into someone else's mind which made you feel powerless to do anything about it.

But it is just thought. It is your thought with an emotion attached to it and you will feel hurt until you stop playing the powerless game. The game that your thoughts are not your own. That is all over now. You are waking up.

Take no thoughts too seriously, before they have been seen from your heart. Choose the thoughts you wish to have and then let them be, let them come easily. And they will as you are more compassionate with yourself and see yourself constantly through the eyes of Your Love.

Be not too attached to any for they will all change as you expand your consciousness.

CHAPTER 70

Stop Scaring Yourself

There is no reason whatsoever to go into worry or be concerned.

Stop scaring yourself.

Everything is in Divine order and will remain that way as you trust and emit only thoughts and feelings of Love and gratitude from your heart.

In these times it is necessary to keep your cool and to continue focussing primarily on your inner journey and the reality of your internal experiencing, on your own alignment for harmony within.

Keep centred wherever you may be and in whatever circumstance and consider everything about human affairs that you see around you as "a movie" that is being played out. It is simply a holographic image created for the benefit of experiencing 3D, it can touch you and it can pull you back into the chaotic quagmire of old mind confusion. You have to continually make the choice to step back (within) otherwise you are allowing it to trigger your old patterns and wounds and to let 3D be the primary directive when you are actually so much More.

There is only the process of renewal which is real and which is for the good of All.

Your True Purpose here is to Know, not as mental knowing but felt as Being Knowing, more of Soul in embodiment that you ARE.

Keep grounding yourself, especially in the sense becoming more at Home with yourself on Earth, just as you are, and your changing body, and you will be connected to the Language of Light, with the energies of the Company of Heaven and your Star Family.

Your calls are always heard and you are always assisted as long as you are prepared to maintain "inner" wakefulness and make constant and frequent connection to your Team.

Never to be afraid again of what is to come. Everything is beautifully worked out in the best interest for all. Your highest good is inevitable if you will it and it is unfolding NOW.

WE are One in our journey and support for each other.

Shine On

CHAPTER 71

We All Have Ever Changing Stories.

Everyone has a story.

I have a sad one and a happy and even comical one, full of the gifts of my experience.

And it all depends whether I am telling it from heart or head, from joy or judgment.

And this is always a choice.

The person I thought I was a little while back when asleep, or who I know I AM now I am awake and Remembering who I truly AM.

PS: Living is all about Heart. Finding the Love within, seeing the "out there" with the eyes of love.

In that seeing is what connects and unifies the outer and the inner.

The world and all its creatures become more amazingly profound.

The Love everywhere reflects you and you are experiencing IT.

And then others around you begin to change (or they fade out of your Now experience).

You are inviting "versions" of them that match your Lovingness. It is felt and known, known and felt, simply by you being who you really want to be and others will be touched by who you ARE. It will call to them who they ARE

It is happening NOW, can you feel it?
Inhale well and feel deeply, sacredly.
Take nothing too seriously.
Take everything into the heart but take nothing "to heart".
You are magnificently HUman.

CHAPTER 72

To Look for Inspiration Daily

Life is not a quest to find yourself and a special place called "Home", for if you are looking for the answer outside yourself then, though it can be an interesting journey, ultimately you will never be content. It may feed you in the moment but you will always get hungry again. Your unfulfilled longing will remain.

There is no quest because there is nothing to find. You have always been here and so you have never been lost.

You have been searching for something that has always been present. You have been searching for the key to unlock the treasure chest of creation and yourself and it has been in "your hands" always.

You just needed to Remember and look.

So your journey is not about finding anything.

It is about REMEMBERING and owning all that is there within you and then Allowing. It is about expansion and experiencing.

Your journey is about enjoying (experiencing joy) the "newness" and exhilaration of the ride for Eternity.

Experiencing every corner, every dimension, every nuance of energy manifestation of the Cosmos, when, where, and how you see fit. Going to Heart, Remembering, and making your Freewill Choices,

And you take it all Home with You. You take who you are and your eternal, infinite connection with You, on a neverending journey of Your own choosing.

You are content, at Home and simultaneously in constant evolution and expansion anywhere.

Contentment is in the knowing of your Place (Home, I AM) and Joy is in the experience of change and growth (expansion), of experience just for the sake of it (because you want to). And it all comes about through Absolute Pure Love of Self at One with All That Is.

And it is this Love. Your love, and the fashioning of it in your life Now, that is creating our New World in the soft, all pervasive, power filled energies of this incoming (Lion's Gate), pink diamond consciousness.

It will be Your love that will lift the whole of humanity up into the LIGHT of our miraculous Now.

Shine On

CHAPTER 73

Living in Your New Reality

FOLKS this is HUGE.

You will change nothing if you do not take the time to really and truly listen within.

How can you experience anything other than what you have patterned yourself to experience unless you drop those old patterns of thought that you are still currently running and allow yourself room to create new thoughts and feelings that enrich you.

COME ON. Stop Fooling Yourself.

You change your thought first and then gather, explore and magnify the feelings you can currently generate that are associated with this new thought into a present moment experience that you can enjoy even though what the thought intends has not fully manifested yet.

You can't just wait for your healing to feel wholeness. You can't wait for your abundance to feel wealthy. You can't wait for the mystical moment to feel awe.

You have to feel awe for the mystical moment to occur. You have to feel love for the new relationship to show up. You have to feel empowered in order to feel success. You have to feel wholeness before your healing can be continuous. You have to feel abundant before your wealth can actually appear.

When your brain and your body change to look like the event has occurred, THAT IS WHEN THE EVENT WILL FIND YOU.

You have to actively engage with your new thoughts daily.

PS: You have new circuitry (crystaline based neurons) waiting right now in our head to be fired through your conscious (5D) Creative thought generation. They require brand new thoughts that are repetitively activated. Thoughts are your PLACEBO for your new state of Being in your body and Creating your experience.

Watch your self talk and consciously begin to change everything that you are telling yourself both in quality and quantity that from your new perspective is absolutely untrue. Watch the Miracles begin to arise.

It is a daily, hourly, minutely commitment and REMEMBERING to You Being YOU.

CHAPTER 74

The Creative Power We have for Good.

What is the meaning of our immense power for good?

We are creating the answer to this question as this next evolutionary move we are making as a Human Collective. As a Remembering Unity Force of Love in Action in the Becoming.

There is just one thought that we have to GET. And that is that we are ONE of the very same Source LIGHT.

And when enough of us get it, really get it, the LIGHT of HUmanity will switch fully ON for All and WE will truly begin to know the tremendous creative power we have for GOOD.

For the Golden Age of Miracles.

It is very near.

Can you Feel it?

It is reality that exists here and Now in your very next moment of choice.

I AM Love incarnate

OR

I cannot feel it yet. The LIGHT is flickering on and off but I do not yet believe it enough to Know it as True, instantly and constantly.

I have not yet fully created or appreciated just how Loving and Lovable I AM.

PS: And how many people will it take? We do not know until WE do it but this birthing of True HUmanity, the Shift, is on track and unfolding perfectly. You have come when you were supposed to come, your life has been what it had to be, and you are poised to express what you are bursting to become and express.

And the (W)hologram will be made manifest by all of us, as Unique sovereign Beings, in tandem with Gaia and all Her realms, our Star Brothers and Sisters and the vast Company of Heaven.

WE will Shift together to our power to Create "GOOD" together. And WE will each create a special vision and version in our own way, expressing our part in the ONE Design.

AND SO IT IS.

CHAPTER 75

To Love Fearlessly

How to handle fear of any kind in this time now.

Fear was never created by you. Fears are prevoked by something external to you. And beyond a certain point of the pain you experience from your fear you have to stop the complaining and end it. Press your own master switch and end it. To let go instantaneously and in that Mastery categorically state "No more".

When you feel fear of any kind at any level say:
"Stop"
Put up a "barrier", an impenetrable wall of your intent of strength around you, and say:
"In the Light of my Knowing, I deny your access at any level in me. Begone".

You are from SOURCE (GOD), a Power that is Indestructible, Eternal, Immutable. No one has power over you, you are Immortal.

Love Fearlessly and no one can have power over you.
They cannot have your fear if you will not receive it.
Rise up in stature.
Stand strong, stand steadfast, stand free.
Feel your push away.
And in whatever else you choose or do, all you have to do is to keep raising your frequency in whatever way you find effective.

Choose to do this frequently, with high intent and your Love for who you are.

Set yourself Free.

CHAPTER 76

Seeking Presence with Others and in Yourself.

Do you sometimes feel a strong pull, to attend this seminar, or that speaker?

Do you have the feeling sometimes that maybe you are missing out on important information or special advancement tools?

Have you attended eagerly awaited events only to come away wondering why you went in the first place?

Of course everything is in its place, but could at least some of this relate to our growing expectation to meet with Soul family. To meet face to face with the kinds of people we have some deeper connection.

To finally begin to physically spend time with others in common Unity (community).

To smile into each other's faces and not see judgement but total acceptance and love, and to hug.

To break bread and "sip wine" together.

To walk along the beach or through the forest together.

To sit in silence together as the sun goes down.

And to sing, dance, and tell stories around a fire in the moonlight.

Is this the confirmation you desire or is it still to attend that special event?

For me there is no contest. I am so happy to be with you here and now dear friends. As I write, you the reader are present. Do you feel it?

This is all coming.

Expect the unexpected Miracles of your meeting with kindred Souls.

The conscious carriers of Light are everywhere on this planet.

You are not alone.

PS: I have only attended only a few workshops in my entire lifetime as a participant, but I have seen so much disappointment and it amazes me how indomitable is the human spirit when moved to KNOW.

And if you came to any of my talks or workshops you would simply learn once again that it is all within You sweet Brothers and Sisters and that you already Know it in the recesses of SELF.

Life teaches me. And only my unwillingness to go to places within, to trust, and follow "my own nose" has caused me pain.

Look no further than in your Heart. And simply follow the Golden markers that are placed out before you every day.

As you become more "at Home with Yourself" you will attract more and more experiences to give you that feeling.

CHAPTER 77

Understanding How You May Affect Others.

Many will have noticed that as you go into places in your joy and lovingness you will be met by opposition, scorn, and sometimes almost fear. Especially where family and 'old friends' are concerned.

They will react, by trying to bring you down, strike out irrationally and want to blow out your Light or run and hide from it.

The most shadowy places are brought to life and into the light of day, the Light of Smile, and through YOUR Loving Presence.

The subconscious in any of us cannot hide any longer.

In the Truth of your Divinity this is the Alchemy and you are the Alchemist. And wherever you are is where you are meant to be.

DO NOT put yourself or the other down nor take a dive again into the pit of hurt, self-pity, blame, confusion, or self-doubt.

The self-pity that says somehow, there is something wrong with you, or how unfair others are. They are where they are as Soul Beings choosing their own experiences.

You may be a trigger but you are not their 'punching bag".

You learn to experience it all in understanding and equanimity but you have choice always and if you would honour yourself when it is necessary you must "speak your piece" in love and then walk away. Not with a feeling of superiority but with understanding for the uneasiness that your comfort and contentedness can engender.

Have Compassion for others and gratitude for your own choices. Perhaps with a little sadness but never with judgement nor regret.

Live wisely and live in joy and gratitude and all things will be added unto you.

CHAPTER 78

Duality as Opportunity to Experience Choice.

Sometimes I have to chuckle to myself when I hear people say that we have to get beyond the reality of Duality (3D).

As if we could?

You are HUman and living in a time of accelerating collective consciousness and of a physical reality in transition.

You came here to experience 3D and you cannot experience it without contrast.

Black/white/, on/off, here/there, this/that, now/then, etc, etc, etc.....

Your mental mind cannot not exist without making a distinction between something and something else.

And as we are evolving, we are Remembering that we are much, much more. And to know that 'More' we have to own that there are other modes of perceiving, knowing and Being, that are beyond conception through mental processing.

However, Being Human requires that we have chosen to experience physicality through this contrast and all the ups and downs of feeling as we meet our experiences.

So it is not about removing duality.

It is about cultivating our "Watcher "

Knowing that we are Soul Beings of mighty awareness and aeons, and aeons and aeons of experience, such that we can stop taking ourselves so seriously because it is all just experience and it is through the contrast and Loving the journey that we make Peace with ourselves and with All Life.

Silly Human.

Don't you Know that you are GOD SOURCE and are Creating this great opportunity to experience whatever you like, whatever will take you back into the depth of Your LOVE. Your Innocent, Compassionate, and Playful SELF and Oh so Powerful BEING.

Your ultimate choice in any given moment is to choose Heart Knowing or the old mental loops of "Right versus Wrong"....

Which do you choose?

LIGHT ON or LIGHT OFF.

PS: I know what I choose and as HUman in a physical world it has to be a constant conscious choice between things. Otherwise, how could I experience my own Freewill?

Life in physicality at the moment without duality experience?!! ..... "Bah Humbug".

CHAPTER 79
On the Way and Always Home

Do you fully realize that the Universe is unfolding perfectly and everything has its place and is in perfect harmony with the whole?

There is a Great Plan of Infinite Benevolence. Only God Knows it, and everyone is included.

You are an essential piece in this Grande singularity. A spinning, pulsating, expanding, luminous field expression of the unified WE. And you have your own Magnificent Filed within it all. And it expands as your Loving embrace of it all Opens Consciously to IT.

Do you get that you are in the perfect place and time ALWAYS?

You create reality to be exactly as you want to experience it. And now you are learning to do this consciously, intentionally and in every moment. What is your Will? What will you imagine, wonder about, contemplate on, feel into, merge with. It is entirely up to you. You have been given total FREEWILL choice.

So you really can relax. You do not have to try anymore to get somewhere. Or be someone Special (You already are). You are there (here really). There is absolutely nowhere better than where you are NOW for who you are and what you are Remembering about you.

You are on Earth recreating "Heaven". Your Home that is there within you wherever you go. Just like the snail.

As soon as you stop trying, guessing, planning, seeking you will immediately begin to see that you already have arrived at that great "final destination" you have been seeking. It has been waiting right with you all the time.

You can unpack all the treasures of Creation from where you are. At Home (content) with yourself.

And it is no final destination at all. It is an unfolding state of Beingness. The bliss, joy, and everlasting peace will instantly show up when you have accepted that you are Home and a HUman Being.

Now the glorious adventure can continue and expand as an entirely Fresh and "new" way. Everything is laid out before you in never ending surprise packages of expansion and joy.

Relax and allow the New Earth Dream to unfold. Allow yourself to create it in this next moment.

CHAPTER 80

Quantum Entanglement

Have you noticed that just as you can flick in and out of 3D, other folks, those you might call "ordinary" and "not awake", those who have not come to the point of glimpsing 5D, of seeking and searching consciously for who they really are, are also beginning to display more 5D type behaviours, more "service to others" acts. They flick in and out of 4D/5D.

And these are not "random acts of kindness". There is nothing random about them.

They are intentional and consciously engaged in with others without "fanfare".

The more you can allow and choose your own 5D being, seeing and doing, the more others will display instances of that same frequency, forward in this 4D reality that you are creating from.

And you wondered how the masses could "wake up".

You create the field frequency and the opportunity for others to choose their own versions of what your grounded Presence emanates.

Along with the curiosity and sense of adventure, to ground more light and Shine, is why you came here.

Everyone who chooses to remain here on New Earth is ascending.

Our Ascension is unique. It is a WE thing.

It is based on the Shining Sacred Heart and the total and complete dedication to unifying thoughts and joy filled expression. The Unity of all aspects of the You with the WE.

Quantum entanglement in a torus field of Lovingness.

PS: And We Give and share because that is our nature, our HUman nature. We see the Gift of Life all the time and thus We no longer look for return because we now Know that Return is the Natural Law of our benevolent Universe. Giving ALWAYS leads to MORE.

CHAPTER 81

The Gift of Sharing.

Have you ever thought of starting a little self-awareness group or some such for people to inspire their self-worth? Have you been prodded but thought you were not good enough not "informed" enough to put yourself "out there"?

For example, on FB, or other social media, there are lots of Friends who might love a chat share, about their visions, hopes and dreams. About their epiphanies, insights, and "penny drops".

Do you ever get a thought or prompt to make contact even if you do not even know them? Do you get a momentary prompt? Can you act you act and trust that insight?

Well I am telling you that self-discovery in this 5th dimensional "approaching", in a dynamic way, is gained through sharing. Your remembering is found in your commitment to be honest and sometimes vulnerable in your "out there".

We all gain from a sincere "echoing" of our Lovingness in the sharing of our own realities (hologram).

It is those you serve who will call to you, and Unity Consciousness is the next "step" in HUman evolution.

Your courage to create your "within" in the "without" is why you came here in the first place. This is what materialisation is all about.

Physical reality has always reflected the "within". You create it. You want the world to change and it is through sharing WE will create it together. Each with our own "version" of it.

It is your "version" of this creation that is a missing piece for US ALL.

As we give of ourselves, guided totally from the "within" of us, we rediscover so many aspects of who we are. Our gift of sharing becomes the unfolding gift of growing, expanding, connecting and Loving. Others magically become our teachers as we offer ourselves to them as "teachers" without boundaries.

With the lightest of heart and the kindness of a prompt, I DARE YOU.

Who knows where it may lead you?

CHAPTER 82

The Rising of Compassion.

Regardless of what appears to be, don't forget.

Maybe it is all a Great Gift.

Maybe you are just being asked to move out of old habits of thinking and seeing and into your peace, and to see the whole human drama (the 3D movie) from your point of compassion and lovingness.

Keep your peace, be your peace and the healing, the resolve, the dissolve of all traumas will become real.

What all the players in the drama are enacting is the duality of separation from Self.

Love them All.

Can you look at trauma/drama, not seeing despair but feeling your compassion, maybe even your tears, and cry for the Love, Honour and Respect of them all.

Yes the so called "victims", but also those who are so lost and afraid that they lash out.

What we are seeing is the last throws of this separateness as all the dross is rising to be cleared in the HUman Heart.

And what you are feeling is the last throws of your own illusionary drama of separation in the collective, and in the experiences of your body that is releasing the toxic effluvia, the unkind lies about the True Nature of HUman and who WE are.

You see, all you have to do is step back into your Love. Hold that ground Lovingness within you for you and the space for the resolution of these things (for all the players and for the healing /transformation of your own body). Tonfeel this on a larger scale so that your compassion knows that Love is the resolution of it all and says "I so love you all, I understand what you are doing, I honour your journey and choice, I Love you and will always Love and honour you, because, like me, you are Love Incarnate".

And to your own body, your compassion for yourself says "I so love you, I understand what you are doing for me, in regenerating, healing. I honour your journey as you have always honoured my choices. I love you and will always love you".

We are transforming ourselves and thus all humanity is being healed through You holding always within you the Honesty to remember all that arises in you and Love the gifts of Knowing that it brings.

CHAPTER 83
Happiness as a Way of Life.

Happiness is not a destination.
It is a chosen state of Being, a WAY of LIFE.
We were never meant to be perfect. So give all that up.
No more 'trying" to do anything (do or not do). Trying to be good, to be "spiritual".
Just be yourself, love every part of being it, and do whatever pleases you, what is fired by your passion (Love).
No more 'serious' stuff even when you are in earnest.
No more second best, only what you want, what fires you up (or brings that gentle, contented glow inside).
From now on it is to be easy and come with ease.
If it doesn't and you still want it just allow it to arise in its own good time. You have chosen it so it can do nothing else but appear.
Shine On
You ARE LOVE INCARNATE.

CHAPTER 84

An Activation: Old Habits Die Hard.

Can you make a Shift?

We have come from a place, and experience whereby we had accepted that basically we had to make our way through a world that was unfriendly. A world that was full of pitfalls and traps, unknowing, and separation.

It did not and could not understand you or who you were. Nor did it want to. You had to fit in but you were given no clear guidelines on how to do it and you could only see the unhappiness of people trying to do it, and those telling you that you had to do it.

BUT, that was a choice. A choice we made to experience when we came here. A Soul Being choice. A choice that as HUman, gave us a feeling of not having much choice.

Now that is all over. We are now Free to choose, though often it does not feel like it.

So what about seeing the whole world (the whole Universe and all Creation in fact), as a totally Friendly Opportunity. You are a Creator Being and it is your Hologram.

To do this you have to be able to look in a different way. A way that comes from the inside to the out, rather than the other way round.

And as WE are more and more experiencing time only as a NOW, only this very moment, and everything around you, in front of you as you sit, your room, and everything in it, on the desk in front of you, or whatever is there, is your friend just as it is. You have actually agreed for this to be your Creation.

It all has consciousness, it all is energy, it has all been provided to you, through your Soul agreement, and expresses the Grace of Being, of existing for you.

It is You, it is connected to you and you are connected to it. You actually created it, as a movie in the energy field of YOU.

So how do you 'make the world 'Friendly'?

It becomes friendly as you feel your gratitude for its being Present. And thus in the simplest way, gratitude provides the bridge to your Freedom, your choice.

It begins to make everything about you friendly, as essential to your now, as acceptable to your now just as it is, without any construction or apparent effort on your part whatsoever. You have chosen to be engage with it otherwise it would not be Present.

Thus from this point of connection to All That Is in your Present moment, you then are free to pay attention to any part of it, or not, because it is now all freely available to you.

So you can now, for example, sit with a group of others, hearing the dramas and the stories and choose to participate, or not, smile within yourself, or not, offer a kind and loving word, or not, stand up and graciously take your leave, or not, etc, etc...... And it is all a beautiful, engaging and unified dance. A friendly, pleasing experience because you have chosen, you are connected, Engaged, and you are friends with it all. And you can recreate it as an experience in any way you choose.

If this resonates you have right this moment made a dimensional Shift. Master Creator that You ARE.

PS: And you can do this self same thing with your feelings because you have access to any thought that you care to choose. So you can choose your victim, powerless, unworthiness stories or you can create its "opposite" simply by choosing opposite thoughts and playing with them.

So you need only think of a young child playing happily and you drop straight onto Heart, from there you can immediately see your world differently .... a Shift.

You recreate it in the LIGHT of your Now Knowing.

Don't make your Enlightenment any more complicated than THIS.

CHAPTER 85
Changing Your Frequency of Experiencing.

Life is all about frequency, and what we are all engaged with at this time is becoming conscious of frequency, learning to Master it within ourselves. Becoming aware of more and more subtle feelings in our Body and Field.

Realising that what is "out there" are events generated by frequencies held "within". That there is an intimate relationship between Field and Form, between within and without, between higher and lower. When we change the frequency within we change the events without, their effect on, and their occurrence. Frequencies that are lower and higher, of the old (Shadow) and of the new (Light).

We are getting use to feeling the waves of energy that are typical of our human experience now, in such a way that we no longer separate the troughs and the crests as "bad" and "good", we drop the stories, the attachments to memories and identities, in other words.

Then we are naturally able, without fanfare, to "neutralize" and raise the "lower" frequencies and blend them with the "higher", the frequencies of Heart.

So realise that low vibration and heavy feeling isn't your fault.

You may not even know it is there or remember how you picked it up. You don't have to know what the resistance is, and you don't have to work at it, analyze it, process it, or suffer. You just feel the feeling, do your small part in allowing it to move through your body and thoughts as emotion (energy in motion), you watch it change peacefully, and Grace does the rest.

You simply feel and allow and your Being, your Divine Presence does the other 90% through Grace.

Just open up to it.

Enlightenment is simply being in the natural Divine Golden Flow of who You are. Shadow fades away in the Light of your Divine Knowing, and with this Knowing you replace the now vacant "space" with your Lovingness. You remove lower Light frequency by creating a vacuum into which higher Light frequency can be streamed in.

When you no longer try to fix anything, and just let go, Grace puts you back in that Flow, and does most of the work (with the help of your High Spirit Team). It naturally, effortlessly paves the way to abundance for you and for those around you whom you touch.

Shine On

PS: And at another level you can accelerate this process by developing a closer, deeper, more intimate cocreative relationship with your Spirit Team (and a specific "higher" guide mentor) who has access to information in your Soul Being (with your freewill permission) that you do not have access to (conscious knowledge of) while in embodiment.

CHAPTER 86

When Your Light Switches On.

There will be a point in your awakening when "the light goes fully on".

Literally, you will close your eyes and you will be often in a Bright Light. Like the lights are full on.

When there is no more doubt and no fear of ever forgetting again.

It has already happened for many of you. We are all already coming from 5th dimensional Beingness but we are still seeing and reacting with the old habits of the 3rd dimension that we feel clearly as denser energies.

As the collective becomes firmly anchored in the 5th, the gifts, the knowing, the gentle euphoria of love, the shift in paradigms, in institutions, beliefs, how we treat one another, and most important of all, how we see ourselves, is changing.

This is the promise of the unfoldment of the Divine Plan.

It is what we have all been working for.

Not that we have been "waiting" because it becomes a totally conscious decision for each of us to BE LOVE NOW.

The more you make conscious choices and are behaving in accordance with your inner nature, and constantly remind yourselves of that decision, the easier and the faster your Shift in the reality you are seeing and sensing, will take place.

Never forget that you are Divine Consciousness, your Auric Field IS Your Mighty Soul Consciousness, you are Love and it is your conscious Lovingness and your willingness to draw in

more Light (which is Infinite Divine CONSCIOUSNESS) that is changing EVERYTHING.
 Shine On

CHAPTER 87

Behind Every Stone is Something New.

People find it so difficult to relax and allow.

Even with all the knowing many are sitting and waiting or still getting caught in "The Search" or caught up in one of the 1001 distractions and narratives being played out everywhere.

But you are "There (Here)" dear hearts. There is nowhere else to go.

The New World, Nova Earth is here unfolding in all Her glory.

You are standing in and with Her. You have arrived through the Great Portal.

Now what do you do?

You wake up. You look about you and start feeling all the old feelings in a new way. You are stretching your "wings" literally. You are exploring your senses, especially in finer and finer feeling. You are sharpening your perception developing a cutting edge. You are Remembering.

You are deciding what you want to create, what brings you more of your deep heart desire to experience, your Joy of being here NOW.

You have the support from your Company of Heaven and the Stars but YOU have to Choose. They will not tell you what you should choose. They wait (not really for they continually pour their various Shine/ LIGHT and Love into our realms) for your next move with so much Love and Confidence in you. You have to ask for specifics, not for materialisations but for the infusion of qualities of your inner characteristic that will enhance you to make strong, clear accurate and decisive choices.

What will you do next.? How will you move into your Shine and prepare the Lighted pathways for All by virtue of How you live?

The New world will show you everything in New Ways.

Behind every stone is something new. Your relationships with others are in total change, Strangers and fleeting encounters are becoming richer in experience, for you are seeing through the facades into Hearts and Souls.

Everything is beginning to reveal its shadows and the secrets, behind and around.

You are the Universe and so everything that is in you and for you is Present. You only have to open your eyes in awe, wonder and with excited and joyous anticipation. To choose, explore and discover through the Eyes of Love.

It is in the eyes of Heart that you are learning to see with and you must be patient and gentle and kind with yourself, for you are as a child, making rediscoveries as if for the first time.

But day to day you have to choose what you want to create and the frequencies you want to create with and experience. Discovering the beauty, harmony and rhythm of the world, as well as within yourself.

You are truly learning to love yourself as you steadily rediscover your World and your Collective. You have all the time in the world so relax, allow and enjoy.

I So Love You.

PS: And for goodness sake STOP taking everything so seriously and personally, and scaring yourself.

PPS: And someone has written to me.

"I feel these words are pushing me to make this final huge positive decision. I feel afraid about it. So have been stalling in the hopes it will happen without my trying. Is to distance myself from someone who I feel is hindering me. Would love to hear back from you Nicky"

We all have the fear when we finally decide to take our Truth first, after eons of stuffing it down. It is fear of the unknown and a background of pain, torture, death, and isolation. But the danger of all this is no longer there. So the pressure will get stronger and stronger until you Jump sweetheart. And when you do the feeling of freedom comes. Love comes, confidence comes.

And if you are willing to follow your Heart, your inner guidance, step by step. Without knowing exactly how it is going to play out.. you will be lead on a fantastic journey to Joy and Abundance.

I kid you not Precious Soul.

CHAPTER 88

No Other Authority Above Your Own Truth.

There are so many "games" being played in the so called "spiritual communities". They are subtle and hidden in what I call "a "shroud" (subtle shadow etheric cloak) of service to others when it is really still with strong elements of service to self.

It is ubiquitous and sneaky both for the other and yourself. You get a kind of "clingy uncomfortable feeling" in its presence. It makes you doubt yourself.

For some a flash of a dark being (entity) is seen and or a feeling like a dagger in your heart. This can be intended in a snap negative thought (judgement) of you or unconscious from the originator (unaware of the shadow hidden in their own Auric field).

It is part of our awakening journey in order to learn to discern what is True in our own Heart and what is masquerading as truth (shadow).

It is rife as we travel through the upper reaches of what is often termed by many as "the 4th dimension.

BE AWARE (beware) that you do not put anyone else's authority above your own "gut feeling" (in contrast to little ego mind story generator).

And the discernment comes from listening to your immediate sense of Heart knowing. And you will always get it though it is quick and in a flash at the very moment of impact of the other.

You are learning to heed it.

This is why I say "First thought is right thought".

It is all about Trusting your own Truth telling.

And mostly you may not know the why about the event or the other person, at first. And you don't need to nor explain yourself to others. Just act on it privately. You learn why on a need to know basis. You are being True to your highest knowing which transcends stories and analysis.

It is so much more about your choice to listen and becoming the Love guided, first responder to your own Knowing.

CHAPTER 89
The Greatness of You Being Here

You are Immense.

You are a SOURCE LIGHT FOCUS for the creative codes of Light to transform matter into crystaline form.

The Divine HUman Genome is a holographic seed "imprint" embedded in the core of your Heart. Everlasting Love as the original seed of You in the "womb of the Mother, The Great Void.

Lovingness is anchored, through you, into every heart that abides on New Earth and beyond. This is why you came here at this time.

You came to ignite the step from lower to higher frequency, in your body, the Divine embodiment of the original seed, and in doing so co create with Gaia, Heaven on Earth.

You came to know shadow in form, and to bring the alchemic power of Lovingness, through you, by making your conscious connection with Gaia and remembering your Divine origin and nature.

You befriend it all through your conscious Love and your conscious Light connection with Creation, however you envisage it. You become whole and create that wholeness in everything you touch.

So even a single thought can anchors that higher dimensional Knowing here and now.

You carry its full potential in your body right Now. That is how powerful you are.

And I remind you that you are not alone and never have been. The Immense Company of Heaven (in all Light frequencies all the way to SOURCE), the great gathering of star Family, Gaia, all creatures and all the dimensional life expressions have gathered very close. The vast array of your Spirit Mentors and helpers are your Friends many of whom have walked the same Diamond Path you are walking.

The veil has gone. They take, with your conscious participation, your loving thought creations and connect and weave your combined projected light codes into a myriad of blueprints for the New Earth within your Auric Field.

You are no longer simply a singular personality, for WE are huge. So dear brothers and sisters remember your connection.

The Great Divine Plan is unfolding now, and each of you is so much an equal partner in it all. And what can you do?

Just Love wherever you are and whatever is before you in this Now moment and all is fulfilled.

Shine On

You are so Loved.

CHAPTER 90

All Our emotions are essential to Being Human

Anger, sadness, loneliness, doubt, confusion, fear, AND excitement, gratitude, peace, happiness, joy, love are my Divine right to experience.

They are an essential part of the experience of my HUmanness.

As I claim and own this experience as my own and as my guides to energetic unfoldment and mastery, the former recede and the latter emanate from the core of who I am.

Claiming it all is part of Loving who I am.

And if I can do this without a story attached to any of it then I am living in the moment making choices between fear and love, between Light off and Light On.

And to claim all emotion without a story, a "clinging to", is to feel it all move through my body, and to experience it as a growing liberation of self. Dancing out of the Shadows.

Grounded in the physical Now, anchored in and through my Heart (the Heart of One).

An experience of unblocking and increasing Flow and fullness of me and All (the WE).

The sweetness, wonder, and beauty of being HUMan.

Be unafraid of any of your feelings.

Allow them, experience them, claim them.

One day you will look back on all these experiences with great affection and delight for HUman Aliveness is a benediction.

You are Divine and you are HUman.

For goodness sake ease up on yourself and all your judgments and enjoy this ride.

PS: And I taste the beautiful freshness of water on my lips and mouth and running down inside me.

I feel the caress of the breeze on my face and in my hair.

I see the beauty and perfection in everything in my vision.

I feel the balance and grace in the movement of my body.

And it is all indescribably delicious

And in this moment there is not one thought I can have that cannot point me to my feeling of Being Alive.

CHAPTER 91

Healing Through Shifting Emotions

All wounds, trauma, dis-ease have an emotional basis.

Someone asks:

"When you are in a very traumatic situation. Does that mean you have to love the situation AND to love the internal feelings about the situation? Or...to bypass those feelings?""

No you feel the feelings that arise and drop the story of why and how you are being wounded, to do this.

What does it feel like in your body as a visceral experience?

When you have done this, really been with what is going on within you, without any judgement of "right or wrong", just allowing it to be Present. You say "Thankyou I see you, I feel you, I acknowledge you, and I honour you. my body, for reminding me".

Then watch as the feeling begins to change or move to different places in your body. If you are simply watching it will begin to CHANGE, to SHIFT to LESSEN even a little.

Then take the opposite feeling. What does that feel like? For example, if it is "sadness" then take "Joy". What thoughts and memories of events bring up that opposite feeling (joy)? How does it (joy) feel in your body when you think of a triggering past experience of it?

You have then generated the feeling you desire to have, that brings you feeling of joy, liberation, excitement.....etc. Sense it, feel it, imagine it. Cultivate it, practice generating it. It will get easier and easier to produce it at will from your intentions to feel it.

You are not suppressing the initial emotional/ physical experience. You are allowing it to run its course through and out of your body and generating the internal "motion" and experience that heals the wounds of the Heart.

As you consciously do this generation of feeling you will then have the place to go when thoughts and feelings of what you do not want are triggered.

This is Complete Healing.

Everything has a frequency of experiencing and we always have the choice.

It is entirely our experience.

PS: A Big Clue: Building a stronger easier, more rhythmic and friendly relationship with Being in your body is a key to being able to run e-motions through your body with greater ease.

Even a regular rhythmic daily "Happy" walk in nature will do the trick.

"Healing" is all about BEING HAPPILY FULLY PRESENT in and with your body.

CHAPTER 92

Feeling More of Who You Are

The Real Secret of becoming More........ Let Go

A huge key to letting go is knowing that life will give you something better than whatever it asks you to give up.

It is the secret of being fearless, of being at peace with yourself. Knowing your own Divine Beingness.

When you realise that life is one beautiful whole movement, a Flow that cannot contradict itself, that is not in conflict with anything it does within itself. That we as human beings, all of us, have the ground of that very stuff within our Soul.

That there is only One person here and that is me/you/us, and so there is no competition, no "haves" and "have nots".

We resist things, we try to control them, simply because we think that life has come to take something away. This was the implant of long ago, it is a downright lie, and you must remove it forever in every twisted belief that is reflected back at you.

And remember often it is the beautiful gift of others to reflect back these twisted images so that you can identify them and choose to let them go.

In a way life HAS come to take something from you but it gives to you always something MORE.

Life comes along to disturb you out of your complacency, and inertia, into new possibilities through your recognition of You as higher being with higher purpose (Potential), as Soul

You. Through the experience of the indescribable Joy of the expansion of your own Lovingness.

First you learn to ignore your doubts and step back from them. Then, seeing the doubts pop up, you choose to Smile and say "I see you, no thankyou". Then you see them float by becoming fewer and fewer and less and less consequential. Eventually they will only impinge if you happen to focus deliberately.

It is your resolute and gentle, subtle and deep intent to be All That You Are, Here and Now. Knowing that life will give you something better than whatever it asks you to give up, is the same knowing you discover when you let go with Love, more of the most exquisite and exhilarating experience of Love, synchronicity, harmony, peace and loving connection flows through and around you. You see it everywhere and all becomes so easy.

IT IS YOU.

I see you Shining.

CHAPTER 93

Pure Love.

Into the Heart of One, the Heart of You

Love is not an emotional attachment or mind possessiveness.

It is the dynamic of Universal singularity.

The energetic/quantum 'Glue' for the behind/within/beyond absolutely everything.

It is both the exhale and inhale, the pulse of expansion and embrace.

And in between is the pause, the stillness, the peace, the absolute bliss of Oneness.

The Infinite, Eternal, Potential for All Creation which IS Love.

Shine On

PS: And let us all move to another level of Love.

Commonly people refer to the unattached Love as "unconditional" but this has subtle limited and a "clinical" unfeeling quality about it.

Does it make any sense to say that there is a "love with conditions"?

So I ask you to say the words "unconditional love" out loud to yourself and feel how it resonates.

Now say "Pure Love" and feel its resonance.

How does it feel?

Does it take you deeper and yet "higher," more expanded.

Pure Love. That is what You ARE.

Becoming More and More

CHAPTER 94

On Living the Dream

By now experiencing the "dream state" in your waking consciousness is becoming very familiar to you.

In the world but somehow removed from it. In a 'haze", unfocussed eyes, and a "far away feeling". Remote from the "matrix" and those still mesmerized and immerse in it.

When the 'I' is fully experienced as in the "Dream" (living and seeing the 3D without being identified as separate in it, a lucid dreaming state that you all are beginning to recognise) and all is embraced in Love through your daily immersion in it, then there is less the difference between "this and that" in terms of separation, on the one hand, and a uniqueness on the other.

What is the difference between 'You and I'. The world that you "used to experience" and the Living Conscious Dream you are now beginning to be immersed in?

And thus we allow the "New reality" to emerge as the natural evolution of HUman consciousness.

Waking up is disabling your old identity and this is where you get confused and frustrated because though you have desires and wants, they cannot be materialised from a point of your old identity. And this is why, though there are still physical requirements to live in 3D you cannot meet them in old ways.

Allowing, letting, go, surrendering and Knowing that the Universe "has your back". Living in "What is the Possibility?' rather than "This is what I must try to do to make it happen."

You really are going to be OK.

So chose to align first with Love and Trust for You whenever you are feeling out of alignment and off balance. Then take the next step with a "Thankyou, Thankyou".

CHAPTER 95

Love Unstoppable

How deeply grateful I am to know that God is everywhere Present. That Divine is everywhere Present.

When I speak of God I am talking about the living God, the God that heals.

SOURCE LIGHT of the purest, lightest, Softest, Strongest qualities you cannot even imagine.

The Love that heals, is everywhere, All the time.

This Love that heals, that is Divine Father, Divine Mother, Divine Friend.

This Friendly energy, this healing energy is right where you are.

And it is UNSTOPPABLE

With a wide open Loving Heart. It is right where anyone is.

It is the Love that connects us

And all this Love needs is a witness.

I witness this Love.

You witness this Love and anyone who reads this can witness this Love

Let us open our Heart and Mind to witnessing Love having its way with anyone. With Everyone.

I call forth robust health, vitality, vigor where You ARE, wherever your children are, your loved ones are, in all areas of your life and theirs.

We align with the nonlinear, multidimensional UNSTOPPABLE joy that bursts us and them All into Being.

We bear witness to this UNSTOPPABLE joy right now.

So BE IT.
And So It Is.

CHAPTER 96

Standing Sovereign Together.

A Question Asked of Me that reflects something many are going through.

"When we choose to stop giving to certain people...do we stop caring for them? I have become so selective towards who I give out my energies to. I am now becoming more energised and have moved from a negative low, to a high that seems so natural. And now I find people listening to me."

Compassion resides in your knowing of the Love that you are. It is your connection to All, so how could anyone be left out of your embrace. It is an ever expanding embrace and not just an energy exchange.

Nothing can be lost because everything is included. Stepping back into yourself is not stepping away from anyone. It is actually the reverse.

Sure you feel a distancing but this is merely the breaking of attachments and hooks and the freeing of yourself and the others to be themselves.

As you let go, surrender, everything comes easier. This is you stepping into your own energetic field. This is You in the FLOW.

Your caring is not in the giving of your energy. It is in the expression of your Self. The immersion in Source (God). Your Sacred heartfelt knowing guiding the Love that you ARE You will feel so different now, in the drawing away from so many people and in the unselfconscious sharing of who you are (your Truth).

It will almost "hurt" in the freedom of it but it will make so much sense. You will be" lifted up" as the Soul You comes Home to your immediate knowing. You "lighten up" in all senses of the phrase. Less is more. No more "trying". Life with the ease that trust brings.

You cannot understand with your mind so you consciously give way to the inner Knowing, the knowing in the feeling of "rightness". You are learning to "see" with the new eyes of the Open Heart. The inner Glow and the outer Shine.

CHAPTER 97

Find and Express Your Joy.

Let me jog your memory.

A Simple Formula Difficult for you to believe.

To the Kitchen Angels, Mothers, Fathers, and Homemakers

You are angels in biological bubbles that you are transmuting to Light. You are here to find and express your joy.

You do it by moving out of fear and into the love that you are?

You do it by making the choices that bring you joy. By taking your courage as a Masters (Mother Stars = "Ma" and 'asters"). By making choices that bring you the feelings of enjoyment, excitement, enthusiasm, and passion.

You do it by letting go of all that does not bring you any of this.

You do it by no longer trying to be the best in terms of how others might judge you, and by forgiving yourself for having been caught up and lost in the experiences that you have chosen to have.

You can easily change them into grateful and expanded feeling of your wisdom of knowing and that are part of your vast reservoir of experiences, simply by going into your Heart and seeing Yourself through your eyes of Love.

You can make new choices now if you dare. Find and feel what you are grateful for right now. Start your day as you sit on your bed before you get up. Say and feel what you are grateful for that you experience now.

Expect miracles of joy coming your way.

Ask for the most benevolent outcomes for you and others who will be in your life today and feel that this is so NOW.

Trust that it will happen, relax all your efforting.

Make your choices during the day with courage and feeling, and trust in the greatness and majesty of who you are becoming. You are an angel, and angels do not make wrong choices. You have never made a wrong choice. Only choices that have led you to greater understanding.

Now that you are waking up your choices do not have to lead to pain anymore when you are seeing more with the eyes of Your Love. But you have to choose and act on those choices. You cannot leave your fate in other's hands. It is unfair to them and demeaning of yourself.

Life is about making the choices, acting them out and having the experience while loving the journey. The rest will follow.

YOUR happiness is the key to provide the happiness you seek for others. And if you can do this for yourself first, you will relax more with your children. The little ones who already come with a knowing that you see clearly when you stop trying to "make it".

They are love incarnate and must learn to feel their own way into life through the experiences they have set themselves. And this will be despite the "best" efforts on your part to protect them from themselves.

Perhaps the greatest gift you can give them is for them to see how someone can be truly happy and free.

Again, you cannot make a wrong choice because you are love incarnate and the center of Your Universe, and it is your view of that Universe which creates your reality.

You are part of a great family and never alone. Remembering that, and knowing it, take the courage of being Yourself.

Do you remember?

Of course you do.

Shine On Mothers and Fathers of the World.

CHAPTER 98

Disengaging from the 3D "Movie".

What you see playing out on the "World Stage" is a "movie" that we have all participated in. A 3D "movie".

What you are experiencing in your version of it is a bifurcation of Shadow and Light. Nothing in the "movie" can be hidden from you.

Shadow and what is in it can no longer be hidden from you.

It cannot operate in the New World reality.

It is being revealed to you for you to make a Choice, in any given moment.

You must first be open to see, hear and Feel it, no matter what it is.

Then you make your Choice.... LIGHT ON or LIGHT OFF.

LIGHT OFF leads back into the "reality" of fear and control.

LIGHT ON leads on into the "reality" of Love and Freedom...A Seeing with the Eyes of your innate Lovingness.

Here is a huge clue for your Freedom

No matter how you see what is happening all around you in your world screen.......

When you actually choose, in a moment of fear, that you are in "a movie", YOU WIN. The game and the power of the "matrix" is over for you, it dissolves.

In owning the fact that you are a Soul Being in a movie, in that moment, you reclaim your power and Shift into a new (parallel) reality.

A whole Evolving Collective Consciousness.
Contemplate this deeply.
It is very simple, but profound in its consequence.
The LIGHT has already won.
It is time to allow the old to unravel and dismantle itself and enact our new choices of Love, Brother/Sisterhood, Creativity, and Community.

Beautiful HUman.

CHAPTER 99
POSTSCRIPT

There is a mighty road and easy road.

And if you have walked the mighty road you are now strong.

And in that strength your Love, your humility and your recognition of the preciousness of all life has lead you to the Truth and Beauty of who you are and what it is to be magnificently HUman.

How else could you be but One of great Compassion and Service because you see and know the you in all?

The you in me, the you in WE.

Shine On

PS: And what became of the easy road?

You now get to choose it every day.

Just go into Heart.

> *You feel Loves Glow.*
> *You walk it now.*
> *The way of Flow.*
> *The path of Allow.*

I So Love You

About the Author

Dr Nicky Hamid (MA., PhD., Dip Tchg.)

Born in London in WWII Blitz, his family immigrated, and growing up in New Zealand, Nicky was inspired and exposed to comparative religion from an early age by his deeply read Theosophist mother who was his pal and mentor.

As a young boy he was mentored in the ancient mystical schools by Masters of the Great Council (known then as "The Great White Brotherhood").

Obtaining a PhD in Psychology in record time Nicky taught at University for 40 years, having written over 100 international research papers, while maintaining a therapy and mentoring practice at the same time. He specialised in Self Awareness, Human Potential and Social Psychology.

He has conducted workshops, `seminars, and Retreats both for children, families, and adults, in NZ, Australia, UK, USA, India, and China. He is an author of 5 books and has posted his writings on Facebook twice a day for 12 years.

He left his long time position as a university Professor of Psychology in order to write, lecture, hold workshops and mentor self-exploration for happiness and wholeness.

He is clairvoyant, clairaudient, and clairgnostic, and has been schooled in both Eastern and Western Mystical traditions all his life by teachers who were not in embodiment. He has seldom attended the workshop of another but has always been shown, through total trust in life experiences, through people who came to him for help, and through "Divine Guidance".

The underlying theme with all he does is with the "touch of love". Nicky heals with words and has always had the ability to read where a person is coming from and what is the next step they could take towards their own happiness.

"I am passionate about self-empowerment and your finding your own connectedness to Creation and to the Source of All That Is.

I have Known since childhood that there would come a time for everyone to wake from their dream of forgetting who they are. The time is at last here and NOW.

The more I know myself.

The less I can define who I am.

I am a different flavour in different circumstances.

I enjoy all my flavours.

But none of them define me. "

Life is a Pandora's box full of surprises and delights when you Master the fact that you always have a choice.

I proudly and humbly own the title my colleagues and students gave me many years ago "Professor of Happiness".

Contact Information

If this book has resonated with you please consider giving feedback and a rating on Amazon. Even a couple of lines would be appreciated. It will so help get this message out there to all who are struggling at this time.

    I write on similar topics almost every day on Facebook. Please consider becoming a subscriber/follower where you can share with a flourishing Soul Family of others around the world. You would be most welcome.

Paperback Books:

All Available on Amazon
https://www.globalmissionoflove.com/books
All You Can Be: Empowering Awakening Angels.
Shift to 5th Dimension: Reminders for Awakening Angels.
Quantum Self Healing: The Power of Coloring Mandalas

Kindle Ebooks:

Simply with Meaning
Freeing the Spirit
All You Can Be: Empowering Awakening Angels.
Shift to 5th Dimension: Reminders for Awakening Angels.
Quantum Self Healing: The Power of Coloring Mandalas
Website: https://www.globalmissionoflove.com
Facebook: https://www.facebook.com/nicky.hamid.5

Readers Note Pad

Chapters to Revisit

Chapters to Revisit

Chapters to Revisit

Insights, Epiphanies, and Felt Shifts

Insights, Epiphanies, and Felt Shifts

Insights, Epiphanies, and Felt Shifts

Notes and Ideas

Notes and Ideas

Notes and Ideas

Printed in Great Britain
by Amazon